The Voyages
of
Ponce de León

Scholarly Perspectives

Compiled and Edited by
James G. Cusick and Sherry Johnson

The Voyages of Ponce de León
Scholarly Perspectives

Cover design by Jackson Walker Studio

ISBN 10: 1-886104-60-3
ISBN 13: 978-1-886104-60-0

The Florida Historical Society Press
435 Brevard Avenue
Cocoa, FL 32922
www.myfloridahistory.org/fhspress

P•R•E•S•S

Publisher's Note

When Juan Ponce de León first visited Florida in 1513, it changed the course of history. The people who had inhabited this land for more than ten thousand years would have their existence forever altered. Ponce's discovery of the Gulf Stream paved the way for the first European colonization of America, and he gave our state its name.

The Florida Historical Society is commemorating the 500th anniversary of the naming of our state by Juan Ponce de León in a variety of ways. A theatrical presentation called *Ponce de León Landed HERE!!* is being presented in historic courtroom venues. Our journal, the *Florida Historical Quarterly*, is featuring a series of special issues on this topic. The theme of our 2013 FHS Annual Meeting & Symposium, held aboard a cruise ship, is "500 Years of *La Florida*: Sailing in the Path of Discovery." We are publishing the book *Paintings by Theodore Morris: Florida & Caribbean Natives* to recognize the diverse people who already lived here when Ponce arrived.

This book, *The Voyages of Ponce de León: Scholarly Perspectives* covers nearly a century of academic research. Editors James G. Cusick and Sherry Johnson have assembled ground breaking articles from back issues of the *Florida Historical Quarterly* along with more recent work by some of Florida's most prominent historians. They have created a book that will endure far beyond the anniversary year of 2013, providing future scholars with valuable information and insight.

The editors have chosen to preserve the previously published articles in this book with their original text intact. This will allow the observant reader to notice how writing and editing styles have evolved over time, as well as how ideas about Ponce's travels have changed and developed. For example, the earliest articles in this collection use the archaic spelling "Porto Rico" which is later replaced by the modern spelling "Puerto Rico." The use of accent marks on Spanish words and the use of italics for non-English words vary among authors and time periods.

The flag of Spain flew over Florida more than a century longer than has the flag of the United States. In 2015, we will be commemorating the 450th anniversary of the establishment of St. Augustine as the oldest continuous European settlement in North America, and Ponce de León paved the way for that colonization to occur. The history of America begins in Florida, with the voyages of Ponce de León.

Dr. Ben Brotemarkle
Executive Director
Florida Historical Society
December 2012

Table of Contents

Introduction

James G. Cusick and Sherry Johnson

In 2013, Florida marks the 500th anniversary of its naming by Juan Ponce de León. Regardless of one's opinion about the course of the subsequent 500 years of Florida history, we feel that it is a good time to revisit the sometimes controversial issues surrounding the voyages of the first documented European to visit Florida in 1513. This collection of essays brings together nearly a century of scholarship about the man, his motives, and his actions. The topics that are explored in this volume include the trajectory of his voyages, the site of his first landing, the purpose of the voyages, the nature of the man himself, and the scholarship that has been written about him over the past century. All the articles in the first section were previously published in the *Florida Historical Quarterly*, but we have also invited contemporary authors to provide essays that exemplify current thinking about Ponce de León and the quincentennial.

In the cutthroat world of the 16th century, Ponce de León was one of many rival explorers fighting for a share of the riches of the New World. His enemies would gladly have displaced him from lucrative appointments, and sometimes did. In legend, however, he became known as the explorer who was searching for the Fountain of Youth and who first characterized Florida as a flowery paradise. The reality was somewhat different. Ponce de Léon came from a family with powerful connections, and gained experience as an explorer with at least one of Columbus's voyages. Despite this, he was forced to leave Puerto Rico because his post as governor of that island was successfully challenged by Christopher Columbus's heirs. In undertaking his 1513 voyage, Ponce de León sought to stake a claim to land he could call his own. In addition, he was probably trying to capture and enslave native people to work in the Spanish settlements of the Caribbean. The native populations of the Caribbean islands were the labor force that fueled Spanish imperial expansion. Disease, warfare, and overwork were decimating this island population, and so demands for additional laborers, captured from neighboring areas, were brutally high. Spanish conquerors had also stamped out attempted rebellions of native groups in the Caribbean. As a man of his time, Ponce de León would not have hesitated to fight with natives in Florida as he tried to establish a beachhead and bring new territory under his control. In all likelihood, his first contacts were with groups along the east coast of Florida, and later with the powerful Calusa kingdom of southwest Florida. His violent confrontation with natives, especially the Calusa, set a pattern for conflicts that were repeated throughout the colonial and territorial periods. In sum, the Ponce de León voyages began a host of changes in Florida that set it on the path to the modern state.

Given the significance of Ponce de León's voyages, and the changes they brought to Florida, it goes without saying that his legacy stirs emotions ranging from pride, to outrage, to sadness for the loss of life on all sides that came about as a consequence. Looking back over 500 years, some believe that Florida has fared fairly well; others will say that it has long been on a disastrous course. But there can be no question that Florida, as we know it, began in 1513. The following essays seek to cast light and provoke discussion about its origins.

The first section of this book consists of articles previously published in the *Florida Historical Quarterly*. Each article reflects its time and collectively they provide a record of how scholarly examination of the de León voyages has changed over the course of the 20th century. They also provide translations from Spanish of many of the key documents associated with Ponce de León. The first example, from 1924, was written by Judge Benjamin Harrison of north-eastern Florida, an early supporter of the Historical Society. Although short, it includes three of the major features that characterize much writing on the topic: an evaluation of primary sources, a fascination with the legend of the Fountain of Youth, and an assertion of the whereabouts of Ponce de León's first landfall. Harrison favored northeast Florida (specifically Atlantic Beach). His text also contains a misattribution for the date of the voyage—1512 instead of 1513—an error that can be traced back to Antonio de Herrera's published account from 1601. This error was a common one in the 19th and early 20th centuries. For example, it is preserved in one of the ceiling mosaics that decorate Henry Flagler's Ponce de León Hotel (now Flagler College) in St. Augustine.

The next article, by T. Frederick Davis from 1932, pursues some of the same objectives, but with numerous emendations. Davis was uninterested in the legend of the Fountain of Youth and largely dismisses it. He also explains why the mistaken voyage date of 1512 appeared in various works. However, most of his article focuses on an English translation of Herrera and what it might reveal about Ponce de León's route and landing. Davis was an avid student of both Caribbean and Florida history. He had worked for the U.S. Weather Bureau in Curacao, and, by the time of this article, had published a history of Jacksonville, Florida. Like Harrison, he concludes that the de León expedition landed in northeast Florida, although he settled on Jacksonville Beach as the most likely location. His abiding interest in the subject is reflected in his 1935 follow up article, a lengthier excursion into source material in English translation. In it, he elaborates on arguments he made in his earlier article, drawing in part on his background with the weather bureau to evaluate evidence for Ponce de León's route to Florida.

The next article comes from Luis Arana, eminent historian for the National Park Service at the Castillo de San Marcos, St. Augustine. Arana, a native of Puerto Rico and bilingual in English and Spanish, was noted for his extensive translations of Spanish documents pertaining to Florida. His discussion of Ponce de León, part of a longer piece on the exploration of Florida, draws on sources unknown or unavailable to Harrison and Davis, identifying, for example, the names of the de León ships. Arana's article is also important for summarizing the principal Spanish accounts about the founding of St. Augustine. This article is followed by another influential one, that of Douglas T. Peck. Using several of the sources cited by Arana, Peck attempted to reconstruct the route of Ponce de León to Florida by re-sailing it. He adjusted his compass bearings to compensate for known errors in compass readings of the 16th century, and he checked his own island landfalls and observations at sea against those reported in Herrera. Peck concluded that Ponce de León probably gained the coast of Florida somewhere in the vicinity of modern-day Melbourne Beach.

In the final of the previously published works, we reprint an essay on the Freducci map of 1514-1515 and its relation to the Ponce de León expedition written by J.T. Milanich and Nara B. Milanich. This intriguing map and its place names adds to speculation about the landfall of the expedition, and, significantly, identifies places in the territory of the Calusa Indians that would recur in later writings about the area.

The second section of this volume brings together three new works on the subject of Juan Ponce de León and his voyages. Eugene Lyon and Brandon Josef Szinável offer a précis about the explorer and his life from a current perspective. They review the first and second voyages, place Ponce de León in the context of his times, and provide detailed information about his family connections. J. Michael Francis then examines the roots of the Fountain of Youth stories, noting that this myth persists, despite being debunked repeatedly by historians, including the contributors to this volume. Francis explains exactly how the myth came into being and reminds us that Florida's history is much richer and more complex than mere legend. Finally, in a major review essay, Amanda Snyder summarizes major articles and books on the subject of Ponce de León and provides an extended bibliography for the use of future scholars. Her essay caps commentary made by Lyon and Szinável, and Francis, and integrates the work of this volume's contributors with other studies.

NOTES ON CONTRIBUTORS

Luis Arana, historian for the National Park Service, Castillo de San Marcos, St. Augustine, translated hundreds of benchmark documents of the Spanish colonial period in Florida. His research and publications became the foundation for reconstruction of military life at the Castillo, and include the collections "Defenses and Defenders of St. Augustine," *El Escribano, The St. Augustine Journal of History* (1999) and "The Endurance of Castillo San Marcos," *El Escribano, The St. Augustine Journal of History* (2004).

James G. Cusick, Curator, P.K. Yonge Library of Florida History, University of Florida, has a background as a journalist, historical archaeologist, and archivist, and writes primarily on the history of Florida. His most recent book is *The Other War of 1812: The Patriot War and the American Invasion of Spanish East Florida* (University of Georgia Press, 2007).

T. Frederick Davis (Thomas Frederick Davis) was born in Chatham, Virginia on April 24, 1877. He spent his early career with the Weather Bureau, then opened an insurance company in Jacksonville, Fla. He always had an interest in Florida's history, and published his best-known work, *The History of Early Jacksonville, Florida*, in 1911.

J. Michael Francis holds the Hough Family Endowed Chair in Florida Studies at the University of South Florida, St. Petersburg. He is a specialist in both Latin American and early Florida history. His books include *Invading Colombia: Spanish Accounts of Gonzalo Jimenez de Quesada's Expedition of Conquest* (Penn State University, 2008) and *Murder and Martyrdom in Spanish Florida: Don Juan and the Guale Uprising of 1597* (American Museum of Natural History, 2011). He has been a research associate at the American Museum of Natural History and the recipient of the 2010-2011 Jay I. Kislak Fellowship from the Library of Congress.

Benjamin Harrison was an early contributor to the *Florida Historical Quarterly* on the subject of Native Americans and Spanish exploration.

Sherry Johnson, Director of Academic Programs, Latin American and Caribbean Center, Florida International University, Miami, writes on social and environmental history of Florida and the Caribbean. She has published several articles in the *Florida Historical Quarterly* on social processes that link Florida to the Atlantic world and on the consequences of hurricanes in the peninsula. Her first book, *The Social Transformation of Eighteenth Century Cuba*, was published by the University Press of Florida in 2001, and her most recent book, *Climate and Catastrophe in Cuba and the Atlantic World* (University of North Carolina Press, 2011) won the Gordon K. and Sybil Lewis Best Book Prize from the Caribbean Studies Association in 2012.

Eugene Lyon is the leading authority on the creation of colonial Florida under Pedro Menéndez de Avilés and a frequently-consulted expert on Spain's colonial maritime empire. A contributor to dozens of scholarly journals and to *National Geographic,* his books include *The Enterprise of Florida, Pedro Menéndez de Avilés and the Spanish Conquest of 1565-1568* (University Press of Flroida, 1976) and *The Search for the Atocha* (Florida Classic Library, 1985). Dr. Lyon directed the St. Augustine Foundation at Flagler College for fourteen years, carrying out microfilming projects in archives in Spain, Cuba, and Minorca. He has been awarded the designation of *Oficial* in the Order of Isabella from King Juan Carlos of Spain and the grade of *Comendador* in the Order of Christopher Columbus from the President of the Dominican Republic, among many other honors.

Jerald T. Milanich, emeritus curator of archaeology for the Florida Museum of Natural History, University of Florida, is the author or editor of more than fifteen major works on Florida history and prehistory, including *Hernando de Soto and the Indians of Florida* (with Charles Hudson) (University Press of Florida, 1993), *Florida Indians from Ancient Times to the Present* (University of Press Florida, 1998), *Florida's Lost Tribes* (with Theodore Morris) (University Press of Florida, 2004), *Laboring in the Fields of the Lord: Spanish Indians and Southeastern Indians* (University Press of Florida, 2004), and *Hidden Seminoles: Julian Dimock's Historic Florida Photographs* (with Nina J. Root) (University Press of Florida, 2012). Dr. Milanich was also co-editor of *First Encounters: Spanish Explorations in the Caribbean and the United States, 1492-1570* (University Press of Florida, 1989), companion volume to a major exhibition on the Columbus quincentenary of 1992.

Nara B. Milanich, associate professor at Barnard College, specializes in modern Latin America. She is the author of *Children of Fate: Childhood,*

Class, and the State in Chile, 1850–1930 (Duke University Press, 2009) and co-editor (with Elizabeth Quay Hutchison, Thomas Klubock, and Peter Winn) of *The Chile Reader* (Duke University Press, 2013).

Douglas T. Peck, a historian of Spanish exploration, drew on published information to re-sail a portion of Juan Ponce de León's 1513 route.

Amanda J. Snyder is a Ph.D. candidate at Florida International University. Snyder earned her B.A. in English and History at Wake Forest University and her M.A. in History at the University of North Carolina Wilmington. Her dissertation, "Pirates, Exiles, and Empire: English Seamen and Atlantic Expansion, 1569-1660," focuses on early modern Atlantic maritime and legal history, and will be completed in April 2013.

Brandon Josef Szinável, a native of Illinois, has worked closely with Eugene Lyon on the family trees and historical records of a variety of Spanish families, drawing on parish records, records of lawsuits, and other historical documentation. Szinável's research includes charting the genealogies of Pedro Menéndez de Avilés and other Austurian families, as well as his own family genealogy. He is a descendant of Christopher Columbus, Juan Ponce de León, and Gonzalo Fernández de Oviedo y Valdés, as well as other Spanish families in Spain's colonial American empire.

Articles from the *Florida Historical Quarterly:* A Retrospective (1924-1996)

Old Pictures of the New Florida, Ponce de Leon and His Land

Benjamin Harrison

July 1924

The discoverers of a new world are accepted as among the boldest and shrewdest men, with very few exceptions; it is the misfortune of Florida that her history is made to begin in popular conception, with her discovery by an old man, who foolishly sought here a renewed youth, that he might gain the love of a young girl. But Ponce stood high among the soldiers and statesmen of Spain, because of the services already given. When he received permission to seek and govern a new land, he was only in the maturity of mental and physical vigor, and if he was weak-minded in supposing it possible to find here a fountain from which youth might be regained, then Columbus was more foolish in accepting a wilder possibility on slighter evidence. If the discoverer of Florida be considered a weak dreamer, then the discoverer of America was a wilder visionary.

Here is an extract from one of the letters of Columbus: "I have always read that the world comprising the land and water was spherical, as is testified by the investigations of Ptolemy and others who have proved by the eclipse of the moon and other observations made from east to west as well as by the elevation of the pole from north to south. But I have now seen so much irregularity as I have already described that I have come to another conclusion respecting the earth, namely, that it is not round as they describe, but of the form of a pear, which is very round except where the stalk grows, at which part it is most prominent. . . . Ptolemy and others which have written on the subject had no information of this part of the world, which was then unexplored; they only established their arguments with respect to their own hemisphere, which, as I have already said, is half of a perfect sphere. . . . I have already described my ideas concerning this hemisphere and its form and I have no doubt that if I could pass below the equinoctial line, after reaching the highest point of which I have spoken, I should find a much milder temperature and a variation of the stars and in the water; not that I suppose that elevated point to be navigable nor (that I could) even find water there; indeed, I believe it is impossible to ascend thither, because I am convinced that it is the spot of the earthly paradise whither no man could go save by God's permission. But this land which your highness have sent me to explore is very extensive and I think there are many countries in the south of which the world has never had any knowledge . . . . There are great indications of this being the earthly paradise, for its sight coincides with the opinions of the holy and wise theologians I have mentioned. And, moreover, the evidences agree with the supposition, for I have never read or heard of fresh water coming in so large a quantity in close conjunction with the water of the sea. The idea is also corroborated by the blandness of the climate. And if the water of which I speak does not come from the earthly paradise it appears to be still more marvelous, for I do not believe that there is any river in the world so wide or so deep."

Now when Columbus deliberately expressed an opinion like this to his sovereigns, was he a foolish old man? Here are his reasons for believing that he had reached the neighborhood of the terrestrial paradise; did Ponce de Leon have reasons equally as good for hoping he might find the fountain of youth in Florida? For the existence of such spring he might quote opinions from all the folklore of all the peoples, but he had individual testimony that might seem convincing. The natives of the islands had told him their fathers had told them of it; he found those who had seen an old man that had visited a country to the west of Hispaniola and come back young; like a sensible man he searched for this example diligently but could not find him, although he heard of his existence many times. Other marvels that would seem incredible had been found in the new world—why despair? So he organized his expedition and set out on his search. He examined the islands as he passed, and always the reports came from the westward; he continued his voyage till he came to Florida.

Where did he land? Let us follow the narrative, not to support, the claims of a particular spot to the honor of this event, but to decide for ourselves as well as we can, what Ponce did and where he went. Let us note that he did not bury his force in a vast and unknown land, as did Narvaez and DeSoto, but acted as a sensible commander should; he was not so carried away by his desire to find his fountain as they were to find gold, but carried his men back home and then went himself to report on his expedition to his king; upon this report the cold and practical King Ferdinand was so well satisfied that he made the captain adelantado of Florida, which was still considered an island, and of the great land of Bimini beyond it. Was Ponce the fool that could deceive the statesmen of Spain and get the commission to exterminate the Caribs at the head of an army and a fleet after his fruitless search for his fountain?

Now let us go with him on his voyage to discover Florida. On March 3rd, 1512, he sailed from the harbor of St. Germain in Porto Rico, skirted the coast of Hispaniola and stretched northward to the Bahamas; he entered the port of Guanahani and asked if anybody knew the way to Bimini or had heard of the fountain of youth. He repaired his ships while he waited, and, having heard no definite tidings of his land or his fountain, he continued his voyage to the Northwest. On Sunday, March 27th, he says he saw land, and later writers declare that all the coast was covered with flowers; Ponce made no such statement. Lowery gives the names of the plants and flowers that Ponce saw, then admits that he made up his list from that furnished by the botanist Bartram long afterward. Now Bartram made a list of the flowers and trees and shrubs that he saw in the valley of the St. Johns; he does not say that any one of these ever grew on the sand dunes that met the eye of Ponce. Yet so began the obfuscation; one writer says Ponce saw what another writer says was elsewhere, and the world holds Ponce responsible for the obvious falsehood! But we know what Ponce saw, for the Atlantic shore of Florida is still what it was then with few exceptions; to a man familiar with the vegetation of the islands, or even with that of Spain a view of the Atlantic shore of Florida would be no more conspicuous for the absence of flowers than for the splendor or the beauty of its appearance. In his report Ponce says not one word about flowers, so far as anybody knows.

Like a careful captain, Ponce watched the shore and sounded the water several days before he tried to land, since he had no harbor. But on April 2 he came close and anchored his ships and went ashore in small boats. He took observations, and says the place of landing was 30 degrees 8 minutes north latitude. We may allow that this was not exactly correct, but he did not enter the mouth of the St. Johns nor the harbor of St. Augustine, for he landed on the open shore, where he found bluffs which we would probably call sand dunes. Somewhere about Atlantic Beach Ponce must have landed, and except for the few houses to be found in that vicinity, we can see now what Ponce saw; can you wonder that he said nothing about flowers?

But he landed on the Sunday known to the church as Pascua Florida, or Palm Sunday, and for that reason he says he named the land Florida, which before had been known as Bimini. He took possession of it for his sovereign, but he saw no Indians; all such trimmings are mere fictions. The inhabitants of these parts were Timucuas, who met all visitors with openhanded generosity and exuberant hospitality, until they were taught by the cruelty of the white man to beware of him; so they received the Frenchmen on the St. Johns and when Menendez landed at St. Augustine they gave him their town and their houses. Why should they be accused of fighting Ponce by later writers?

After landing Ponce sailed along the coast, back and forth, but he does not say that he saw any people or any flowers, though we may easily suppose that he landed occasionally. The Timucuas were not foolish enough to offer him worship nor savage enough to attack him; no doubt they watched him and wondered, but he saw them not. Then Ponce sailed southward, doubled Cape Canaveral, which he described, and passed some time among the keys; he tells about the birds and turtles; we remember him still in his name for the Tortugas. He had trouble with the winds and the currents, and he doubled the cape and sailed up the west coast, but he was not fool enough to lose himself in an unknown country like Narvaez and DeSoto. Then and there he gave up his search for the miraculous fountain; when next he came it was to found a settlement and govern a land that seemed fair and good. So he determined to go home, but he left one of his ships, and an old woman he had found on a key with Juan Perez de Ortubia to continue the search. To Ponce in Porto Rico came Ortubia and told him of Bimini that he had seen, which was large, verdant, with crystal springs in abundance, and covered with beautiful groves, where, however, he did not find the fountain of youth; Was Ponce deceived into further search? Not he; Ortubia talked to his heart's content, but Ponce went off to Spain, made his report, received the empty honors his king gave for such services, and accepted a commission to conquer and settle the land he had discovered. Also he sailed at the order of the king to exterminate the pirate Caribs who had fought him and made themselves a terror and a pest in all those seas. Here is presented the photograph of the real Ponce de Leon, who has been transformed into all sorts of a fool by those who made of him a hook on which to hang their own imaginings; who in their little way desired to play the part of Cervantes and took the unfortunate old knight for their Don Quixote.

One other case. Years after when men should have known more about Florida, the Captain General, Pedro Menendez, met with one, Fontaneda, who had been taken from a ship wrecked in the straits of Florida and had spent some years among the Indians. From this man the great and wise Menendez sought information, and he thought Fontaneda a man well worthy of credence and respect. So Fontaneda wrote an account of his observations and experiences, which was sent to Spain as information, and there filed among the archives of the Council of the Indies, where it may be found to this day—a state paper considered by bishops, statesmen and soldiers worthy of such care. Did a man like Hernando D'Escalante Fontaneda consider it impossible that a water might be found in Florida that would restore a man's youth? Here is what he says on the subject, without exciting incredulity from the men of his time, whether in Florida or in Europe:

"Juan Ponce de Leon, believing the reports of the Indians of Cuba and San Domingo to be true, made an expedition into Florida to discover the River Jordan. This he did, either because he hoped to acquire renoun [sic], or perhaps because he hoped to become young again by bathing in its waters. Many years ago a number of Cuban Indians went in search of this river, and entered the province of Carlos (in South Florida), but Sequence, the father of Carlos, took them prisoners and settled them in a village where their descendants are still living (1568). The news that these people had left their own country to bathe in the River Jordan spread among all the kings and chiefs of Florida, and, as they were an ignorant people, they all set out in search of this river, which was supposed to possess the power of rejuvenating old men and women. So eager were they in their search, that they did not pass a river, a brook, a lake or even a swamp, without bathing in it, even to this day they have not ceased to look for it, but always without success. The natives of Cuba, braving the dangers of the sea, became the victims of their faith, and thus it happened that they came to Carlos and built a village. They came in such great number that, although many have died; many are still living there, both old and young. While I was prisoner in those parts I bathed in a great many rivers, but I never found the right one."

Now, isn't it time that we do justice to an old soldier who fought hard and lived as he could but was nobody's fool? He never said Florida was a land of flowers; he located the place of his landing according to his best knowledge. The picture of his floral landing is drawn from the fancy of others; when we hear of his wandering in swamps to bathe in the mud along with the alligators, the eye is that of Fontaneda, who said not a word of Ponce in that connection.

Now what is the fact behind these stories of a Fountain of Youth? Since we cannot believe that age can be rejuvenated, was there a Fountain of Health, whose fame might have been confused by transmission through different dialects and languages into the miraculous by credulity and ignorance?

Modern science has learned beyond dispute that every chapter of folklore is based upon some fact; everyone has something solid and substantial behind it. Columbus was right in looking towards the east for his terrestrial paradise, for now we know that our first civilized ancestors had transformed with their canals and irrigation works the land between the rivers into a Paradise, from which had sprung the empires of Assyria and Babylon and Ninevah—every drop of blood in the veins of Columbus directed his imagination to the America which was then hid from mortal vision.

Investigation has proved that parties accompanied the sick to the springs of Saratoga before the first white man had seen America, but the pioneers of New York and New England were not interested in native traditions. In the South the predominant native race was that of the Muscogee, and there is ample proof that its tribes once held a great part of the Mississippi Valley. There is abundant evidence that parties accompanying the sick were privileged to pass through even the hostile tribes to the Hot Springs of Arkansas, and these came from distant lands, being allowed to hunt and maintain themselves on the way. Since the sick passed, we must believe that some were restored to health; why should not the fame of such recoveries pass down into Florida and on to the islands? All the reports of the fountain pointed to the North; parties such as those mentioned by Fontaneda may have wandered till they despaired and then returned to live with the Caribs, who held the fringe of the South Florida coast.

From some of the diseases found by the Spaniards to be prevalent among the Indians, the Hot Springs of Arkansas are still prescribed; accept the legend as that of a Fountain of Health, and we have evidence that the basis of truth has been found. Now in the old papers on the subject the two terms are used alternately and interchangeably—the miraculous waters for which Ponce de Leon sought really existed, and he has the laugh on his critics.

The Record of Ponce De Leon's Discovery of Florida, 1513

T. Frederick Davis

July 1932

The Fountain of Youth Myth

In the time of Columbus there was a tradition among the Indians of the West Indies that toward the north was a land called Beniny (Bimini), where all manner of delights could be found. Our knowledge of this comes solely from a letter to the Bishop of Rome, written by Peter Martyr, a contemporary of Ponce de Leon, as follows:[1]

> Among the islands on the north side of Hispaniola [Haiti] there is one about three hundred and twenty-five leagues[2] distant, as they say which have searched the same, in which is a continual spring of running water, of such marvellous virtue, that the water thereof being drunk, perhaps with some diet, maketh olde men young again. And I here must make protestation to your holiness not to think this to be said lightly or rashly, for they have so spread this rumor for a truth throughout all the court, that not only all the people, but also many of them whom wisdom or fortune hath divided from the common sort, think it to be true; but, if you ask my opinion herein, I will answer that I will not attribute so great a power to nature, but that God hath no lesse preserved this prerogative to himself than to search the hearts of men . . .

Probably Ponce de Leon, who had lived some time in the West Indies, knew of this tradition, but his opinion of it we do not know. It is certain, however, that it was not the lure that induced him to embark upon the voyage which resulted in the discovery of Florida. All that is known of this voyage is contained in two primary or source records, namely: The patent

---

[1] Peter Martyr, D.2, C.10, Lok's Trans. See *Early Voyages to America*, Virginia Historical Society, Richmond, 1848, p. 206.

[2] A Spanish sea league was about 3 miles.

authorizing him to go in search of the legendary island of Beniny, signed in Spain by the king on February 23, 1512,[3] and the account of the voyage itself by the great Spanish historian Herrera,[4] who is thought to have had access to the original notes or log-book (now lost) of Ponce de Leon.

The Source Records

The patent authorizing Ponce de Leon to make the voyage sets down clearly the objects sought. It is to be a search for gold and other things of material value; and if these were found specific provision was made for the crown's share. The Indians were to be apprehended and apportioned as slaves among the explorers under the direction of the king. The mines were to be worked in the manner of those of Hispaniola, that is to say, by Indian slave labor. There is not a sentence in the whole patent that conveys the most remote impression of romance; it was a clear-cut direction to search for those things that occupied the attention of the world of that day. And under this patent Ponce de Leon sailed from the island of San Juan (now called Porto Rico) in March, 1513, to find the island of Beniny.

The account of the voyage is contained in Herrera's *Historia de los Hechos de los Castellanos* (1601), Decada I, Libro IX. That part relating to the-discovery of Florida and the voyage down the east coast will be found in Cap. X, pp. 301-303. The following literal translation is taken from Dr. L. D. Scisco's *The Track of Ponce de Leon in 1513*, published in the *Bulletin of the American Geographical Society* for October, 1913, because the translation is carefully made and also because it is later referred to in this account:

> Juan Ponce de Leon finding himself without office, through Juan Ceron and Miguel Diaz having been restored to those of the island of San Juan, and seeing himself rich, determined to do something with which to gain honor and increase estate; and as he had news that lands were found to the northward he resolved to go to explore toward that part; for which he equipped three vessels, well supplied

3   For an English translation of this patent see *American Catholic Society Record*, December, 1912; translation by L. D. Scicso.

4   Antonio de Herrera (1559-1625), who is generally accepted as the primary source on Ponce de Leon's first voyage to Florida.

with provisions, people and seamen, which for the purpose of exploring are most necessary.

He sailed from the island [San Juan] on Thursday, in the afternoon, on the 3d of March, setting out from the harbor of San German. He went to Aguada, in order to take from there his course. The night following he sailed to sea, to northwest a quarter by north, and the vessels proceeded eight leagues of a day's run, until the sun rose. They went on sailing until on Tuesday, the 8th of the said month, they came to anchor at the banks of Babueca, at an island that they call El Viejo, which is in twenty-two and one-half degrees [latitude]. Next day they anchored in an islet of the Lucayos called Caycos. Presently they anchored in another called La Yaguna, in twenty-four degrees. On the 11th of the same month they reached another island called Amaguayo, and there they were at stop for repairs. They passed on to the island called Manegua, which is in twenty-four and one-half degrees. On the 14th they reached Guanahani, which is in twenty-five degrees and forty minutes, where they prepared one vessel for crossing the weatherward gulf of the islands of the Lucayos. This island Guanahani was the first that the admiral Don Christoval Colon [Columbus] discovered, and where, in his first voyage, he went on land and named it San Salvador. They set out from here, running northwest, and on Sunday, the 27th, which was the day of the Festival of the Resurrection, which commonly they call 'of Flowers', they saw an island and did not examine it. And Monday, the 28th, they ran fifteen leagues by the same direction, and Wednesday they proceeded in the same way, and afterward, with bad weather, until, the 2d of April, running to west-northwest, the water lessening to nine fathoms at one league from land, which was in thirty degrees and eight minutes, they ran along the length of coast seeking harbor and at night they anchored near the land in eight fathoms of water. And thinking that this land was an island they named it La Florida, because it had a very pretty view of many and cool woodlands, and it was level and uniform: and because, moreover, they discovered it in the time of the Flowery Festival [Pascua Florida] Juan Ponce wished to conform in the name with the two facts. He went on land to take information and possession.

On Friday, the 8th, they made sail; they ran in the same direction, and Saturday they sailed to the south a quarter by southeast; and sailing by the same rhumb up to the 20th of April they discovered some huts of Indians, where they anchored. And the day following, all three vessels proceeding along the edge of the sea, they saw a current such that, although they had a great wind, they could not proceed forward, but backward, and it seemed that they were proceeding well; and in the end it was known that it was in such wise the current which was more powerful than the wind. The two vessels that found themselves nearest land anchored, but the current was so great that the cables went tight, and the third vessel, which was a brigantine, that found itself more to sea, must have not found bottom, or did not know of the current, and it drew it away from land, and they lost it from sight, the day being clear and with fair weather. Here Juan Ponce went on land, called by the Indians, who presently tried to take the boat, the oars, and the arms. And in order not to break with them it was permitted them, in order not to cause irritation in the region. But, because they struck a seaman in the head with a staff, from which he remained unconscious, it was necessary to fight with them, who, with their arrows and armed shafts—the points of sharpened bones and fish-spines—hit two Spaniards, and the Indians received little hurt. And the night separating them, Juan Ponce re-gathered the Spaniards with hard work. He set out from there to a stream where he took water and firewood, and stayed awaiting the brigantine. Sixty Indians repaired there to hinder it. One of them was taken for a pilot, and so that he might learn the language. He put on this stream the name of La Crux, and he left by it one [i.e. a cross] hewn from stone, with an inscription. And they did not finish taking water, because of being brackish.

On Sunday, the 8th of May, they doubled the cape of La Florida, which they named Cabo de Corrientes, because the water ran so much there that it had more force than the wind, and did not permit the vessels to go forward, although they put out all sails. They anchored behind a cape close to a village called Abaioa. All this coast, from Punta de Arracifes [point of reefy islands] as far as this Cabo de Corrientes extends north and south a quarter by southeast, and it is quite clear and of depth of six fathoms; and the cape is in twenty-eight degrees and fifteen minutes. They sailed on until they found two islands to the south in twenty-seven degrees. To one that had a league of extent they put the name Santa Marta. They reached water in it. On Friday, the 13th of May, they made sail, running along the coast of a sandbank and reef of islands as far as the vicinity of an island that they named Pola, which is in twenty-six and one-half degrees, and between the shoal and the reef of islands, and the mainland extends the open sea in the form of a bay [Biscayne Bay]. On Sunday, the day of the Festival of the Holy Spirit, the 15th of May, they ran along the coast of rocky islets ten leagues, as far as two white rocky islets. And to all this line of islands and rocky islets they put as a name Los Matires, because, seen from a distance, the rocks as they raised to view appeared like men that were suffering."

Ponce de Leon continued to cruise among the islands and reefs of the lower Florida peninsula. He sailed some distance up the west coast, and finally, backtracking, again reached the Bahama Islands, where he dispatched one of his to continue the search for Beniny, himself returning to Porto Rico in October, 1513. In due time the other vessel reached Porto Rico, after having discovered a well-wooded and watered island (probably Andros Islands); but the riches sought were not there, nor the spring that "restores old men to youths." The only reference to the Indian tradition in the whole narrative was in connection with this vessel's supplementary voyage, and it has the ear-marks of an after-thought.

Review of the Voyage

Ponce de Leon's course from Porto Rico to the Florida coast was constantly northwesterly. He sailed along the islands and shoals that form the eastern fringe of the Lucayos, now called the Bahamas. He mentions a number of islands whose names are still familiar, but he gives them latitudes different from the present. From this fact discussions have arisen as to the accuracy of Ponce's readings, and attempts have been made to apply corrections. The jackstaff had come into use by that time, and with it approximately correct observations were possible under favorable conditions. The pitching of a ship in a heavy sea would make accurate readings much more difficult. The method of calculation had likewise improved. So there is no reason to doubt the possibility of determining approximately correct position in fair weather and with the exercise of care.

We cannot say positively that the islands mentioned by Ponce were the ones so named today. Many changes in place names have taken place since that day. His supposed incorrect latitudes fit other near-by islands, and it is not impossible in some instances, being a stranger there, for him to have mistaken their identity. His reading for San Salvador,[5] for instance, is applicable to Eleuthera, and it is not impossible that that island was Ponce's San Salvador. Every contributing circumstance, and many are necessary, must positively be known before a correction in sliding ratio could rightly be applied; further, the meaning of the accompanying text must be preserved. While interesting, such results cannot be accepted as fact. The most elaborate discussion of this kind is that of Dr. Scisco,[6] but in applying his assumed correction, Ponce de Leon is made to sail due west from the Bahamas to the Florida coast when he says he sailed northwest, with the result that many features of the text are entirely upset.

Ponce de Leon headed northwest after leaving his San Salvador. On Easter Sunday, March 27, he saw a coast which he took to be that of an island. On Wednesday, the 30th, still sailing northwest, he ran into a storm and for three days struggled against a "northeaster" as this sort of weather is called on this coast. At this time he was almost certainly in a latitude north of Cape Canaveral, which roughly marks the southern limit of influence of northeast weather resulting from an area of high pressure over the North Atlantic at this season of the year-which must have been the condition he met. The natural wind sequence following a northeaster here would be veering through southeast and south to west. As soon as it got to southeast the sea would begin to calm, and between south and west, being an off-shore wind, the surf would be quiet. The wind had probably gotten into the south by April 2d, when Ponce headed in west-northwest toward the coast. At one league from the shore he began to take soundings, where he found nine fathoms of water, exactly as it is today according to U. S. hydrographic maps. This was in latitude 30° 8', which is the only observation of his whole voyage that he seems to have taken with especial care, the others being usually to the nearest half degree.

---

[5]   Both Watling's Island and Cat Island have been designated as the San Salvador of Columbus, as well as two other islands. See chart in Justin Windsor's *Christopher Columbus*, 1892, p. 210.

[6]   "The track of Ponce de Leon in 1513" in *Bulletin of the American Geographical Society*, October, 1913.

The Landfall

Laid down on the modern map, a point on the beach in latitude 30° 8' is about eleven miles south of Pablo Beach[7] and eighteen miles north of St. Augustine. That locality is the nearest recorded point to Ponce de Leon's landing place, though the exact spot where he went ashore and took formal possession may have been a short distance north of it. From Herrera's text it is indicated that they headed in west-northwest toward the beach; that they came within a league (3 miles) of the shore, took their latitude, made soundings, and sailed along the beach looking for a place to anchor. When night overtook them they anchored eight fathoms of water, at less than three miles off-shore. It is here Ponce went ashore and took formal possession. The place could not have been far north of the point where the observation 30° 8' was taken. Judging the average sailing distance on fair days to have been about two miles an hour, and applying this average to the six hours sailing time[8] in the afternoon of April 2, the anchorage was somewhere off Pablo Beach. While this seems to be approximately correct and confirms the circumstances of Herrera's record as well as the hydrographic conditions of today, we must still consider the positive record of 30° 8' latitude as designating historically the locality where Ponce de Leon landed and formally claimed the "island" of Florida in the name of Ferdinand, his king.[9]

The coast that Ponce de Leon saw is well described by Pedro Menendez Marques, who, writing to the king in 1573, said:[10] "All this coast [he was describing the coast between Cape Canaveral and the mouth of the St. Johns River] is composed of sandy beaches and groves of trees, and at most points from the topmast one can see inland rivers, which are arms of salt water, which appear about half a league within the country; and one can anchor all along this coast, where there is no side [east] wind."

Ponce de Leon anchored in eight fathoms or 48 feet of water, a circumstance prohibiting the acceptance of the claim that he entered a harbor before anchoring. All of the inlets or harbors on this part of the coast were

---

[7]   Pablo Beach is now called Jacksonville Beach.

[8]   Observations for latitude were taken at noon, leaving at that season about six hours before dark.

[9]   Sometimes it is stated that possession was taken for "Ferdinand and Isabella" but this is wrong, as Isabella had been dead more than eight years when Ponce discovered Florida.

[10]   Jeannette Thurber Connor's *Colonial Records of Spanish Florida*, Florida State Historical Society, 1925, Vol. 1, pp. 325, 327.

shut in by shoals and sandbars, navigable only with the greatest caution through intricate shifting channels. Had Ponce made the attempt, he most likely would have wrecked his ships; but even had he been successful in the hazardous undertaking, nowhere would he have found 48 feet of water, or anywhere near that depth. We may be certain, therefore, that he anchored off the beach, where he said he anchored.

There is nothing in the record to indicate that Ponce de Leon saw the St. Johns River. It is reasonably certain that had he seen it, the largest river he had ever seen up to that time, he would have noted it, judging from the things he did mention. Nor did he see the ancient Indian town Seloy, located on the site of the present St. Augustine, because the only inference that can be drawn from the record of Herrera is that the first habitation and the first Indians he saw was after he had turned back and sailed far down the coast, where the Indian hit his sailor on the head with a stick-and there started a war that lasted more than three hundred years.

What Ponce did during the five days he lay anchored off the place where he first went ashore is not known. He saw neither Indians nor any indications of gold or other precious metals. Consequently the main objects of his voyage were not here. He was probably occupied with mending his sails and rigging, which must have needed attention as the result of the storm through which he had just passed.

Apparently there were no priests with the expedition, and so the ceremony of taking possession was without the softening influence of religious participation. Probably it was a short and formal ceremony. The scene is not that of surpliced priests kneeling in prayer amidst the banners of the Church, but rather one of a little group of hardy explorers gathered on the beach somewhere about half way between St. Augustine and the mouth of the St. Johns River, representing the coming of the white man to the mainland of North America-an event that foretold the expansion of one race at the expense of another.

The Year of Discovery was 1513

Early historians, excepting perhaps only the Inca Vega[11] and later Peschel,[12] followed the marginal entry 1512; appearing in the Herrera record

---

[11] Garcilaso de la Vega, *Conquest of Florida,* Madrid, 1723.

[12] Oscar Peschel, the German historian, writing about the middle of the nineteenth century.

as the year of Florida's discovery by Ponce de Leon. This was done until sometime in the 1880's, when a research worker in analyzing the circumstances of the voyage saw that it was impossible for the patent signed Spain on February 23, 1512, to have reached Ponce de Leon in Porto Rico in time for him to equip his vessels and sail by March 3d, following. Then began a wide-spread discussion and investigation by historians and historical magazines. Ponce de Leon was accounted for during most of the year 1512 in and around Porto Rico. A check was made of the date Easter, March 27, and it was found that March 27, 1512, was not Sunday at all, but a week day; however, it was disclosed that March 27, 1513, was Sunday and Easter Sunday, too, and that the other dates mentioned in Herrera's narrative were proper for that year. The year 1513 was at once accepted as the correct date, the assumption being that the date 1512 was originally a scribe's or a printer's error. George R. Fairbanks, the eminent Florida historian, used 1512 in his earlier works, but in the later editions he changed it to 1513. The year 1513 is now given by all historians as the year of Ponce de Leon's discovery of Florida.

Likewise, considerable confusion is occasioned by the use of Palm Sunday for Easter Sunday to designate the season of the discovery of Florida by Ponce de Leon. Washington Irving used Palm Sunday in his *Voyages of the Companions of Columbus,* and he was followed by Fairbanks to the end; but Herrera's text states plainly "Pascua Florida", which means the Feast of the Resurrection, sometimes called the Festival of Flowers, which is Easter. Just how or when the use of Palm Sunday in this connection originated is not known.

History of Juan Ponce De Leon's Voyages to Florida: Source Records

T. Frederick Davis

July 1935

PREFACE

On that day between the 2nd and 8th of April, 1513, when Juan Ponce de Leon stepped from his landing boat upon the sandy shore of Florida he opened the positive history of the white man within the limits of the present United States. Since then, through the centuries, his name has been perpetuated by history and is better known today than any of the early explorers with the single exception of Columbus. But the circumstances of his discovery of Florida are seldom related with historical accuracy, while those of his second voyage to colonize Florida are scarcely known at all. This is due in large part, without doubt, to the inaccessibility of the original Spanish records and the dearth of English translations of them. The purpose of this work is to provide accurate translations of these source records in full, that the student of American history may have before him under one cover all that is known historically concerning Ponce de Leon's two voyages to Florida.

In presenting my conclusions I have in every case given my reasons therefor. They were derived from an extensive study of the subject for the sole purpose of finding the true story in the original records themselves as published herein. It differs in many respects from the popularly accepted version of Ponce de Leon's association with Florida, and hardship and disappointment supplant the customary picture of romance; but it is none the less interesting from a historical standpoint, because the courage of pathfinders is real, while historical romance is usually fiction.

I have derived both satisfaction and pleasure from this study, the former from having found a, virgin field for original research, the latter because of the sincere interest shown by many-the kind of encouragement that means much in any earnest effort. My gratitude is here expressed to all, and specifically to those who gave their time and talent as a contribution to this work, namely: C. L. Crow, James A. Robertson and Florence P. Spofford for their authoritative translations of source records; Charles B. Reynolds, for valuable suggestions and the loan of rare material in his possession; Kenneth A. Friedman and T. Hurd Kooker for the well-drawn maps; and Carl Bohnenberger, Emilio Carles, Alston Cockrell, Alexander J. Mitchell and Eugene M. Sanchez for help in various ways.

Jacksonville, Florida
May 15, 1935

PONCE DE LEON'S FIRST VOYAGE AND DISCOVERY OF FLORIDA

The Records

Juan Ponce de Leon, after serving in the armies of Spain, embarked for the West Indies where he became active in the subjugation of the Indians, a service in which he was engaged many years. He was a soldier and led a military life until he was forty-five years of age or more. He appears in official civil life with his appointment as governor of the eastern part of Hispaniola (Haiti), known as the province of Higuey. Soon afterward he was appointed governor of the island of San Juan (now Porto Rico), which he had already partially explored and conquered from the Indians. This office he held until relieved (c. 1511) without prejudice, as a result of the decision of the Council of Spain to favor others, principally the heirs of Columbus, for the high positions in the West Indies. Hitherto, Spanish exploration had been directed south and west of the West Indies, but rumors had become current that lands had been found toward the north. Yielding to the wanderlust that possessed these early Spaniards, Ponce asked permission of the King to explore in that direction.

The *capitulacion* or patent granting the authority for the voyage of discovery will be found in *Documentos Ineditos del Archivo de Indias*, XXII. 26. The translation of this patent was rendered for me by Dr. James Alexander Robertson, author of many standard historical works and internationally known as an authority on Spanish-American history. Presented here directly from the pen of Dr. Robertson the reader is assured of having before him a, correct interpretation of this important Ponce de Leon document.

The Patent

Whereas you, Juan Ponce de Leon, send to entreat and beg as a favor from me that I grant you permission and authority to go to discover and settle the Islands of Beniny, under certain conditions which will hereafter be declared, therefore, in order to show you favor, I grant you permission and authority so that you may go to discover and settle the island aforesaid, provided that it be not one of those already discovered, and under the conditions and as shall hereafter be set forth, as follows:

Firstly, that, with the ships you wish to take at your own cost and expense you may go to discover, and you shall discover, the island aforesaid; and for it, you may have three years' time counted from the day on which this my patent shall be presented to you, or when the contract shall be made with you in regard to the settlement aforesaid, provided that you shall be obliged to go to discover within the first year of the three years aforesaid, and that on going you may touch at any islands and mainland of the Ocean Sea, both discovered and to be discovered, provided they be not among the islands and mainland of the Ocean Sea belonging to the very serene king of Portugal, our very dear and very beloved son; and it is understood that you may not take or possess any profit or any other thing from them or any of them lying within the limits stipulated between us and him beyond only the things which should be necessary for your maintenance and provision of ships and men, by paying for them what they should be worth.

Item, That you may take, and there shall be taken on your part in these kingdoms of Castile, or in the said Isla Espanola, for the abovesaid, the ships, supplies, officers, sailors, and men that you should find necessary, by paying for them in full according to custom, in the presence of our officials in Isla Espanola at present residing and who should reside in our House of Trade thereof, and in Castile, in the presence of our officials residing and who should reside in our House of Trade of Seville.

Item, In order to show you favor, I order that during the period of the three years, no person may go, nor shall he go, to discover the island of Beniny aforesaid; and if any one should go to discover it, or should discover it by accident, the stipulations of this my patent shall be carried out with you and not with the person who should thus discover it; and if another discover it, you shall lose nothing of the right which you have therefor, provided that, as aforesaid, you should set sail to go to discover it within the first year aforesaid, and that it will be of no value in any other way ; and provided that it be not one of those of which report and certain knowledge is had.

Item, That when you find and discover the island aforesaid in the manner abovesaid, I make you the gift of the government and justice of it for all the days of your life, and for it I give you full power and civil and criminal jurisdiction, with all their incidences and dependencies, and annexes and rights.

Item, That when you find the island aforesaid, as abovesaid, you shall be obliged to settle at your cost in the sites and places that you can best do it; and that you may have possession of the houses and farms and settlements and hereditaments that you should make there, and of the gain you should have in the island aforesaid, in accordance with the provisions of this contract.

Item, That, if fortresses should have to be built in the island aforesaid, they must be and shall be at our cost, and we shall place therein our wardens, as we should see best fulfills our service; and if, while the forts aforesaid are being built, you should build any house or houses for habitation and for defense from the Indians, these shall be your own; and if there should be need thereof for our service, you shall have to give them on being paid their value.

Item, That I shall give you, and by the present I do give you, for the space of twelve years, counted from the day on which you should discover the island of Beniny aforesaid, the tenth of all the revenues and profits belonging to us in the island aforesaid, if this is not from the tithes of our profits or in any other manner whatsoever.

Item, That the allotment of the Indians who should be in the island aforesaid, shall be made by the person or persons who should be appointed by me, and in no other manner.

Item, That I shall order you, and by the present I do order you, that the Indians who should be in the island aforesaid, shall be allotted in accordance with the persons there should be [in your expedition]; and that this be observed and that the first discoverers be provided for before any other persons; and that all the preference that should conveniently be shown in this be given to them.

Item, That I grant for the space of the ten years aforesaid that those persons who should go to discover the island aforesaid and who should settle on that voyage, enjoy the gold and other metals and profitable things which should be in the island aforesaid, without paying us from them other fees or tithes the first year; in the second, the ninth part; in the third, the eighth part; in the fourth, the seventh part; in the fifth, the sixth part; and the other five years after that paying the fifth, in accordance with and in the form and manner in which it is now paid in the Isla Espanola; and that the other settlers who should go later, who are not included among the discoverers should pay the fifth from the first year; for I order another exemption to be given to the latter instead of that from gold.

Item, To show greater benefit and favor to you, the said Juan Ponce de Leon, it is my will and pleasure that you are to have the government and settlement of all the islands lying near the island of Beniny aforesaid which you should discover in your person and at your cost and expense in the manner aforesaid, and which are not among those islands of which information is had, as abovesaid, under the conditions and in the form that is set forth in this my agreement ; and as, by virtue thereof, you are to have of the island aforesaid.

Item, That I grant you the title of our adelantado of the island aforesaid, and of the other islands you shall discover in the manner aforesaid.

Item, That you collect the gold, if there should be any, in the same way in which it is now collected in the Isla Espanola, or in the form and manner that I shall order.

Item, That you can not take in your company, for the aforesaid, any person or persons who are foreigners from outside our domains and seigniories.

Item, That for assurance that you, the said Juan Ponce and the persons who should go with you will execute, carry out, and perform and that the contents of this patent which it pertains to you to observe and carry out shall be carried out, performed, and observed, before making the said voyage shall give trustworthy and creditable bonds to the satisfaction of our officials residing in the Isla Espanola.

Item, That you, the said Juan Ponce, and the other persons who should go and remain there, shall execute and observe and perform all that is contained in this my said agreement, and every part and parcel of it, and you shall not cause any fraud or deceit, nor shall you give favor, or aid or consent thereto; and if you should learn of any, you will inform us and our officials in our name, under penalty that any person of you who should do the contrary, by that very fact he who does not so act, shall have lost any grace or benefit which he should have from us, and shall pay in his person and goods all the penalties which we should consider it fitting to order executed on the persons and goods of those who should do it, or consent to it, or conceal it.

Item, That after having reached the island and learned what is in it, you shall send me a report of it, and another to our officials who reside in the Isla Espanola, so that we may know what should have been done and take the measures fitting to our service.

Therefore, if you, the said Juan Ponce carry out all the abovesaid and every part and parcel of it, and shall have given the said bonds or give and pay the things abovesaid, I promise and assure you by the present to order everything contained in this patent and every part and parcel of it to be observed and carried out, and order our officials who reside in the Isla Espanola that in our name, in accordance with the abovesaid, they should make the said contract and agreement with you and receive the said bonds. For your despatch, I am ordering Don Diego Colon, our admiral and governor of the said Isla Espanola, and our appellate judges and the officials of our treasury who reside there, and all the justices of the said Isla Espanola that they give you all the favor and aid that you should find necessary, and that no impediments be offered you therein or in any part or parcel of it.

Done in Burgos, February twenty-three, one thousand five hundred and twelve.

I the King

By command of his Highness
Lope Conchillos.
Sealed by the Bishop of Palencia.

Source Authority

Antonio de Herrera (1559-1625). In 1592, Philip II of Spain appointed Herrera to the position of official historiographer of the Indies. His monumental work *Historia General de los hechos de los Castellanos en las Islas i tierra firme del Mar oceano* appeared in 1601 and contained an inexhaustible mine of facts relating to early Spanish activities in America. *In it is the only account giving the details of Ponce de Leon's voyage and discovery of Florida.*

His official position allowed him access to original and secret papers, many of which have since been destroyed no doubt.

Although Spanish historians prior to Herrera mentioned the voyage of Ponce de Leon, their accounts are vague and inaccurate in many particulars and appear to have been partly founded on hearsay. Herrera seems to have had before him the original notes or possibly the report Juan Ponce was required to make to the King, now believed to have been destroyed. Now and then a document is found having a bearing upon the voyage, but it is very improbable that an authentic contemporaneous record will ever be discovered which will materially alter Herrera's account. In the original (1601) edition the account is in Decada I, Libro IX, Caps. X and XI, pp. (311) 301-305.

I have two translations of Herrera's account in full, made by experienced translators competent to render old Spanish correctly. They vary in style; but are exactly alike in interpreted meaning. The translation used here is by Florence P. Spofford, who rendered it directly from the 1601 edition of Herrera in the Library of Congress.

Herrera's Account, 1512[1]

Juan Ponce de Leon, finding himself without office, on account of Juan Ceron and Miguel Diaz having been restored to those of the island of San Juan, and seeing himself rich, determined to do something by which to gain honor and increase his estate; and as he had news that there were lands to the northward, he resolved to go to explore toward that part; for which he armed three vessels, well provided with food, men and mariners, which for the purpose of discovery are most necessary. He sailed from the island Thursday, in the afternoon, the 3rd of March, setting out from the harbor of San German. He went to Aguada, in order to set from there his course. The night following he went out to sea; northwest a quarter by north, and the vessels went eight leagues of a day's run, before the sun rose. They sailed on until on Tuesday, the 8th of the said month, they came to anchor at the banks of Babueca, at an island that they call El Viejo, which is in twenty-two and one-half degrees [latitude]. Next day they anchored in an islet of the Lucayos called Caycos. Soon they anchored in another called La Yaguna, in twenty-four degrees. On the 11th of the same month they reached another island called Amaguayo, and there they remained for repairs. They passed on to the island called Manegua, which is in twenty-four and one-half degrees. On the 14th they reached Guanahani, which is in twenty-five degrees and forty minutes, where they made ready one ship to cross the Windward gulf of the islands of the Lucayos. This island Guanahani was the first that the admiral Don Christoval Colon discovered, and where, in his first voyage, he went

---

[1]   Herrera's running-head date. Modern historians use 1513 as will be explained later.

ashore and named it San Salvador. They set out from here, running North-west, and on Sunday, the 27th, which was the day of the Feast of the Resur-rection, which commonly they call [the feast] 'of Flowers', they saw an island but did not examine it. And Monday, the 28th, they ran fifteen leagues in the same direction, and Wednesday went on in the same manner, and afterward, with bad weather, until the 2nd of April, running West-Northwest, the water diminishing to nine fathoms, at one league from land, which was in thirty degrees and eight minutes [latitude], they ran along beside the coast seeking harbor, and at night anchored near the land in eight fathoms of water. And believing that this land was an island, they named it La Florida, because it had a very beautiful view of many and cool woodlands, and it was level and uniform; and because, moreover, they discovered it in the time of the Feast of Flowers [Pascua Florida], Juan Ponce wished to conform in the name to these two reasons. He went ashore to get information, and take possession. On Friday, the 8th, they set sail, running in the same direction: and Saturday they sailed to the South a quarter by Southeast; and keeping the same course until the 20th of April, they discovered some huts of Indians, where they anchored: the day following, all three vessels following the seacoast, they saw such a current that, although they had a strong wind, they could not go forward, but rather backward, and it seemed that they were going on well; and finally it was seen that the current was so great it was more powerful than the wind. The two vessels that found themselves nearest the land anchored, but the current was so strong that the cables twisted; and the third vessel, which was a brigantine, which was farther out to sea, could find no bottom, or did not know of the current, and it was drawn away from land, and lost to their sight, though the day was clear with fair weather. Here Juan Ponce went ashore, called by the Indians, who immediately tried to take the boat, the oars, and the arms. In order not to break with them, they suffered it [not wanting] to cause trouble in the land. But, because they struck a seaman in the head with a stick, from which he remained unconscious, they had to fight with them; they, with their arrows and armed shafts-the points of sharpened bones and fish spines-wounded two Spaniards, and the Indians received little hurt. The night separating them, Juan Ponce re-gathered the Spaniards after hard work. He set out from there to a stream where he took water and firewood, and stayed awaiting the brigantine. Sixty Indians went there to hinder him. One of them was taken for a pilot, and so that he might learn the language. He gave this stream the name of La Cruz and he left by it a cross hewn from stone, with an inscription; and they did not finish taking water, because it was brackish. On Sunday, the 8th of May, they doubled the cape of La Florida, which they named Cabo de Corrientes, because the water ran so swift there that it had more force than the wind, and would not allow the ships to go forward, although they put out all sails. They anchored behind a cape close to a village called Abaioa. All this coast from Punta de Arracifes as far as this Cabo de Corrientes runs north and south a quarter by southeast, and it is quite clear with a depth of six fathoms; and the cape is in twenty-eight degrees and fifteen minutes. They sailed on until they found two islands to the south in twenty-seven degrees. The one having an extent of one league they named Santa Marta, and there they found water. On Friday, the 13th of May, they hoisted sail, running along the coast of a sandbank and reef of islands as far as the vicinity of an island that they named Pola, which is in twenty-six and one-half degrees, and between the shoal, the reef of islands, and the mainland, the open sea extends in the form of a bay. On Sunday, the day of the Feast of the Holy Spirit, the 15th of May, they ran along the coast of rocky islets ten leagues, as far as two white rocky islets. To all this line of islands and rocky islets they gave the name of Los Martires because, seen from a distance, the rocks as they rose to view appeared like men who were suffering; and the name has remained fitting, because of the many that have been lost there since. They are in twenty-six degrees and fifteen minutes. They continued sailing, sometimes to the North and at other times to the Northeast, until the 23rd of May, and on the 24th they ran along the coast to the south (not trying to see if it was mainland) as far as some islets that extended out into the sea. And because it appeared that there was an entrance -between them and the coast for the ships, in order to take on water and firewood they stayed there until the 3rd of June, and careened one vessel called the San Christoval. And at this time Indians in canoes repaired there to reconnoiter the Spaniards for the first time. They saw that the Spaniards did not go ashore, although the Indians called them when they raised an anchor to repair it and they thought that they were going away. They put to sea in their canoes and laid hold of the cable to carry away the ship; for which the bark was sent among them and, going ashore, they took four women and broke up two old canoes. At other times when they repaired there they did not come to a rupture, because they saw no disposition [toward it] but they traded skins and guanin [low gold]. On Friday, the 4th, while awaiting wind to go in search of the chief Carlos, as the Indians on the ships said that he had gold, a canoe came to the boats; and an Indian who understood the Spaniards, who, it was believed, must be from Hispaniola or from another island of those inhabited by the Spaniards, said that they should wait, as the chief wished to send gold in order to trade. And while waiting there appeared at least twenty canoes, and some fastened together by twos. Some went to the anchors, others to the ships, and began to fight from their canoes. Not being able to raise the anchors they tried to cut the cables. An armed bark was sent against them and made them flee and abandon some canoes. They took five and killed some Indians and four were captured. Two of them Juan Ponce sent to the chief that they might tell him that notwithstanding they had killed a Spaniard with two arrow wounds he would make peace with him. The following day the bark went to sound a harbor that was there, and the party went ashore. The Indians arrived and said that the next day the chief would come to trade (but it was a deception). Meanwhile the people and canoes gathered together, and at 11 eighty men in breech-clouts appeared on the ship that was nearest. They fought from the morning until the night without hurt to the Spaniards, because the arrows did not reach them, while on account of the crossbows and artillery shots they dared not draw near, and in the end the Indians retired. The Spaniards after having stayed nine days, on Tuesday, the 14th, resolved to return to Hispaniola and San Juan, with the intention of discovering on the way some islands of which the Indians that they carried gave them information. They returned to the island, where they took water, and they named it Matanca, from the Indians that they killed. On Wednesday they went in search of the eleven rocky islets that they left to the west. On Thursday and Friday they ran in the same direction until, on Tuesday, the 21st, they reached the rocky islets, which they named Las Tortugas, because in one short time in the night they took, in one of these islands, one hundred and sixty tortoises, and might have taken many more if they had wanted them. They took also fourteen seals, and there were killed many pelicans and other birds that amounted to five thousand.[2] On Friday, the 24th, they ran to the southwest a quarter west. On Sunday they sighted land. On Monday they proceeded along the coast, in order to examine it, and on Wednesday they made harbor thereon and dressed the yards and sails, although they were unable to learn what country it was. The greater number considered it Cuba, because they found canoes, dogs, cuttings from knives and from iron tools; and not because anyone knew that it was Cuba, but by the argument that for Cuba they took that course, and that it ran east and west like it, except that they

---

[2] That is to say, of the five thousand birds on the island they killed many.

34

found themselves eighteen long leagues off the route for it to be Cuba. On Friday they set sail from here in search of Los Martires. On Sunday they reached the island of Achecambei, and passing by Santa Pola and Santa Marta, they reached Chequescha. They sailed as far as some islets that are on the shoals of the Lucayos more to the west, and anchored on them on the 18th of July, where they took on a supply of water. And they gave to them the name La Vieja, from an old Indian woman that they found, and no other person. They are in twenty-eight degrees. The name that La Florida had in the beginning could not be learned in the opinion of its discoverers, because, seeing that that point of land projected so much they considered it as an island; the Indians, as it was the mainland, gave the name of each province and the Spaniards thought that they were deceiving them; but in the end, because of their importunities, the Indians, said that it was called Cautio, a name that the Lucayos Indians gave to that land because the people of it covered certain parts of their body with palm leaves woven in the form of a plait. On the 25th of July they set out from the islets on the lookout for Bimini, ailing among islands that seemed water-swept. And, being stopped, not knowing by what way to pass with the ships, Juan Ponce sent the bark to examine an island that he considered overflowed and found it to be the island of Bahama. So said the old woman that they carried with them, and Diego Miruelo, the pilot, whom they met with a bark from Hispaniola that was going on its own venture, although others say that by luck they had made port there. They set out Saturday, the 6th of August, by the route they had been following, and until finding the depths they ran Northwest a quarter West as far as an islet of rocks alone at the edge of the depths. They changed course and ran by the edge of the shoals to the South. They changed this course next day, although Bimini was not in that direction. And for fear of the currents that another time were driving the ships to the coast of La Florida or Cautio (as they then called it) they took up their return route for the island of San Juan de Porto Rico. And having sailed until the 18th of August they found themselves at daybreak two leagues from an island of the Lucayos, and ran three leagues, as far as the point of this island, where on the 19th they anchored and stayed until the 22nd. From here they delayed four days in arriving at Guanima, because wind and passage failed them. And they turned back from its coast to the island of Gautao; and by storms they were kept engaged there without being able to go from it twenty-seven days, until the 23rd of September. And the bark from the island of Hispaniola that had joined them was lost there, although the people were saved.

Having overhauled the vessels, it appearing to Juan Ponce that he had labored much, he resolved, although against his will, to send some one to examine the island of Bimini; for he wished to do it himself, because of the account he had of the wealth of this island, and especially of that particular spring so the Indians said that restores men from aged men to youths, the which he had not been able to find, by reason of shoals and currents and contrary weather. He sent then, as captain of the ship, Juan Perez de Ortubia, and as pilot Anton de Alaminos. They carried two Indians for pilots through the shoals, because they are so many that one proceeds with much danger because of them. This ship departed on the 17th [27th?] of September, and Juan Ponce the next day for his voyage. And in twenty-one days he arrived within sight of San Juan and went to make harbor in the bay of Porto Rico; where, after having found Bimini, although not the spring, the other ship arrived with the account that it was a large island, cool, and with many springs and woodlands. The discovery by Juan Ponce of La Florida so ended, without knowledge that it was the mainland; nor for some years thereafter was that assurance obtained.

Review

Early maps. Several maps purporting to antedate Ponce de Leon's voyage of 1513 have been found that may be interpreted as crudely outlining the south Atlantic and Gulf coasts of North America, with a projection in the relative position of Florida. Of chief interest among them is the Cantino map, supposed to have been made in 1502. These maps have been widely discussed by eminent historians and cartographers. Some are of the opinion that they are the product of a mapmaker's fancy; others, that they may have been intended to represent the popular conception of another coast, and all treat their authenticity with more or less caution. A voyage of the character indicated would have in that day excited the civilized world to such an extent that a record of it or some reference to it would certainly have been preserved somewhere. No account of any kind, printed or in manuscript, is known. We should naturally suppose that among the early writers one would have had knowledge of such a discovery and would have indicated it; but all give the credit of Florida's discovery to Ponce de Leon, and until it is proven by authentic source record that the white man had been here before he will continue to be credited by history with the honor.

Nautical aids. At the time of this voyage several devices were in use *for ascertaining latitude.* They were correct in principle, but in practice great care was necessary for accurate results. These devices were designed for zenith (noon) observations only; consequently, when the sun was obscured at noon no readings could be taken with them. Evidently some method was in use for estimating the *speed of vessels.* The *compass* had been perfected and its variations were known and understood. Serviceable under all conditions, it was the navigator's main reliance at sea. Sailing directions recorded by these early voyagers therefore cannot be questioned for instrumental error. Fortunately Herrera gave Ponce de Leon's sailing directions minutely and they are of the utmost importance in a study of the voyage.

Purpose of the voyage. According to an Indian legend of the West Indies there existed an island called Bimini[3] (supposed by the Spaniards to be one of the Lucayos, or as we call them now, the Bahamas), which contained a "spring of running water" having the quality of restoring youth to the aged; and to this lure the usual modern account attributes Ponce de Leon's voyage. When we recall that Juan Ponce, still within the zone of the prime of life at 52, had spent years fighting these Indians and was familiar with their characteristics, it is rather difficult to comprehend his expenditure of a large part of his fortune in an expedition just to verify their tradition. His patent authorized him to explore for Bimini and other lands. In the first sentence of his account Herrera states with unmistakable clearness that as Juan Ponce had knowledge that lands had been found to the northward he resolved to go to explore in that direction. This was the main objective of the voyage. The lands to the northward referred to could have been none other than the Cabot and the Cortereal discoveries of the Labrador and Canada coasts, to which the fishermen of Europe afterward found their way and the rumors of which by the process of slow dissemination had sifted through to the West Indies. This fact is partly indicated by the patent prohibiting Juan Ponce from encroaching upon the discoveries of Portugal-the only Portuguese discovery in the north up to that time was that of Cortereal.

---

[3] Bimini is spelled Beniny in the patent to Ponce de Leon.

The First Voyage

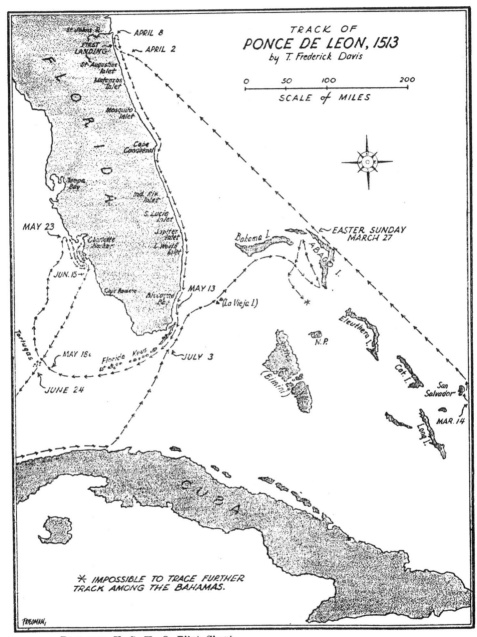

Base map U. S. H. O. Pilot Chart.

The Discovery of Florida

(The following extract from Herrera's account is repeated here for emphasis and easy reference. It is *the only historical record* concerning Ponce de
Leon's actual discovery of Florida and the place of his first landing, what he
did there and why he named the land Florida. The interpolations in brackets
are mine.)

This island Guanahani was the first that the admiral Don Christoval Colon [Columbus] discovered, and where, in his first voyage, he
went ashore and named it San Salvador. They set out from here, running Northwest, and on Sunday, the 27th [March], which was the day
of the Feast of the Resurrection, which commonly they call [the feast]
'of Flowers', they saw an island but did not examine it. And Monday,
the 28th, they ran fifteen leagues in the same direction [northwest],
and Wednesday went on in the same manner [northwest], and afterward [northwest], with bad weather, until the 2nd of April, [when]
running West-Northwest, the water diminishing to nine fathoms, at
one league from land, which was in thirty degrees and eight minutes
[latitude], they ran along beside the coast [northerly] seeking harbor,
and at night anchored near the land in eight fathoms of water. And
believing that this land was an island, they named it La Florida,
because it had a very beautiful view of many and cool woodlands, and
it was level and uniform: and because, moreover, they discovered it
in the time of the Feast of Flowers [Pascua Florida], Juan Ponce
wished to conform in the name to these two reasons. He went ashore
to get information, and take possession. On Friday, the 8th, they set
sail, running in the same direction [northerly]: and Saturday they
sailed to the South a quarter by Southeast; and keeping the same
course until the 20th of April, they discovered some huts of Indians,
where they anchored . . .

Florida was not discovered on Easter Sunday. A northwest course from
San Salvador, the course that Juan Ponce held, would pass close to and in
sight of the island of Abaco, the northernmost of the Bahamas, and the first
land that would be seen after leaving San Salvador. It must be remembered

that this was long before the invention of the telescope and the low-lying islands to the westward (Eleuthera and Cat), 35 miles away, would not have come into eye view. The land that Ponce de Leon saw on Easter Sunday, March 27, could not possibly have been the Florida coast as generally believed, because the coastal trend between Palm Beach and the mouth of the St. Johns River is NNW and the NW and WNW course held by the vessels during the six days between March 27 and April 2 would have carried them across the peninsula into the Gulf of Mexico. It would appear certain, therefore, that the island Juan Ponce saw on Easter Sunday was Abaco Island, and further indication that this is true will be shown later.

The bad weather. The vessels ran into "bad weather" the fourth day out from Abaco Island. They were then (estimated from their average sailing speed of two miles an hour as determined presently) some seventy-five miles off Cape Canaveral and near or in the Gulf Stream. "Bad weather" is a relative term and does not necessarily signify a storm; in another place Herrera uses "storm" in its proper sense. The season was too early for tropical hurricanes, and too late for continental cyclones that drift northeasterly across the United States to have a material effect upon the weather as far south as Canaveral. The "bad weather" was evidently the result of an area of high barometric pressure over the north Atlantic—a frequent condition in the spring causing thick weather off the Florida east coast, often, but not always with strong winds. The ships were not scattered, indicating moderate winds. The Gulf Stream in weather like this is usually "choppy" and doubtless bounced the vessels around considerably, justifying the term "bad weather." The failure of Juan Ponce to mention the Gulf Stream at this time, as he did later on in his voyage down the east coast, was because he could not detect it under such conditions. The wind sequence off the Florida northeast coast as the result of weather of this kind would be northeast, veering gradually through east to south and south-west, usually requiring three days to make the half circle at that season. Thus it is probable that while Ponce de Leon tacked for a time against a side wind, it soon veered to a favorable wind and [on] April 2 when he reached the Florida coast he found an off-shore wind and a moderate surf.[4] I have seen the ocean here like a lake with practically no surf running for several days at a time with light to moderate offshore winds.

Herrera's latitudes. At the time of this voyage the astrolabe method of ascertaining latitude had been supplemented by the cross-staff. They provided only for noon observation. The device was held in the hand and angles obtained by direct eye observation, a method requiring a steady nerve and stable base for accurate results. Mariners sometimes went ashore for especially accurate work, as observations with these devices on a pitching or rolling vessel were obtained with extreme difficulty and often resulted in considerable error.[5] Such errors are called "accidental" to distinguish them from instrumental errors. The latitudes assigned by Herrera to those islands of the Bahamas that can now be recognized (supposedly) are not true latitudes, which has led to discussions and attempts to derive a correction to be applied to all of the latitudes mentioned in the account under the assumption that all were wrong. A general correction for accidental errors is impossible of determination; and a correct instrumental error could be found only after a series of perfect observations at each location under exactly similar conditions. In other words, it cannot be done; and besides, to change all of Herrera's latitudes in proportion to the apparent errors for the Bahamas would produce situations irreconcilable to the meaning of the proven text. Herrera records a total of ten latitudes as follows and in the sequence named:[6] 22 ½°; 24°; 24 ½°; 25° 40'; 30° 8'; 28° 15'; 27°; 26 ½°; 26° 15'; 28°. When judged carefully six of these ten latitudes have every appearance of being simply approximations or dead-reckoning; three are in doubt; and only one, the 30° 8' landfall of Ponce de Leon on the Florida coast, has the earmarks of a carefully obtained instrumental reading, which may have been checked by him on shore.

The latitude 30° 8' plays an important part in all of the discussions concerning Ponce de Leon's discovery of Florida. The expression "those old latitudes" is often used, which creates in the mind a doubt as to the possibility of ascertaining true latitude in the time of this voyage. Strange to say no one has attempted to analyze the circumstances in support of the record in this specific case, and to this end let us now examine the circumstantial evidence for a check on the accuracy of the 30° 8' record of Herrera.

---

[4]   Based on the author's own knowledge of weather conditions on this coast derived from long service as an official of the U. S. Weather Bureau at Jacksonville.

[5]   Justin Windsor, *Christopher Columbus*, 1892, p. 260.

[6]   One degree of latitude here is approximately 68.9 statute miles.

Circumstantial Verification

The northwest sailing course from San Salvador. A northwest course from San Salvador passes close to Abaco Island and reaches the Florida coast near or slightly above the mouth of the St. Johns River. It is the course that Herrera says Ponce de Leon held until April 2, when he turned to west-northwest and at noon (when observations for latitude were taken) was approaching the coast. From Abaco Island the distance is about three hundred and twenty-five miles, which he sailed in six days more or less, or at a rate averaging around two miles an hour. This is what might be expected of vessels of their type in the open sea under varying weather conditions. As they changed course on April 2, and were in sight of land at noon, it follows that they sailed not more than half a day in the new direction. There being only a slight change in direction, northwest to west-northwest, the distance short and the speed slow, the landfall could not have possibly been many miles below the point where they would have reached the coast had they continued the original northwest direction. From these facts it can be easily determined that the contact must lie between St. Augustine Inlet and the mouth of the St. Johns River. Herrera records that it was in 30° 8' latitude. True latitude 30° 8'; is almost exactly half way between St. Augustine Inlet and the mouth of the St. Johns.

Hydrographic conditions. Storm waves have undoubtedly caused some erosion of this part of the coast since Ponce de Leon's time, but the tendency is to build up again during intervals. The projecting point at the mouth of the St. Johns River on the south side shown on the earliest maps and mentioned in early records was where the sand fields and dunes near the south jetty are now building up. This point was originally a ridge of high sand dunes with some wooded growth, shutting out the view of the river to a vessel approaching from the south, even from the topmast, until it had rounded the point. In any case, along the beach the shelving or depth of water would remain relatively the same. Herrera records that in latitude 30° 8' Ponce found nine fathoms of water three miles off shore, and modern hydrographic maps show the same.

No harbor where Ponce landed. Coming in nearer than three miles, Ponce sailed up the beach looking for a, harbor, but he did not reach the St. Johns

River, as he certainly would have noted a river of that size; nor did he find any other harbor, as his anchorage in eight fathoms, or about 48 feet of water proves. Even with the aid of modern dredging operations there is no such depth of water as that at either St. Augustine or in the St. Johns River. The complete omission of coastal details from Herrera's account indicates that there were none to record, which fits exactly the situation where he says Ponce's landfall was. Ribault, the first to visit this part of the coast after Ponce de Leon, verifies these facts in the report of his voyage. Coming up from the direction of St. Augustine Inlet, Ribault anchored Thursday, April 30, 1562, close under the projecting point on the south side of the St. Johns, of which he wrote as follows:[7]

> And because there appeared to us no sign of any port, about the setting of the sun, we cast anchor again, which done, we did behold to and fro the goodly order of the woods wherewith God hath decked everywhere this land.[8] Then perceiving towards the north a leaping and breaking of the water,[9] as a stream falling out of the land into the sea, forthwith we set again up sail to double the same [the point] while it was yet day. And as we had done so, and passed beyond it, there appeared to us a fair entry of a great river, which caused us to cast anchor again, and tarry near the land, that the next morning we might see what it was.[10]

There is nothing in Herrera's account to indicate that Ponce de Leon's anchorage was off a river or inlet or inside a harbor; to the contrary the inferences that can be drawn from it all point the other way.

The Indians. The patent under which Ponce sailed gave detailed instructions as to the Indians that might be found. They were one of the main objects of the voyage and it is natural that he should note them wherever he saw them, which he seems to have done. Failure to mention them at the first landing place consequently indicates that no Indians were found there. This

---

[7]   See Jeannette Thurber Connor's *Jean Ribaut,* 1927, p. 65.

[8]   Note that Ribault also mentioned the woodlands that entered into the naming of Florida by Ponce de Leon.

[9]   Caused by an ebbing tide over the shoals and sandbars at the mouth of the river.

[10]   This was the discovery of the St. Johns River. Ribault named it 'River May, because he actually entered it on the 1st of May. It was among the last of the great sea-flowing rivers of North America to be discovered by white men.

in turn indicates that the landing was neither at the site of St. Augustine nor at the St. Johns River, because at both of these points, as later recorded by the French and the Spanish colonizers (1562-65), there were found established Indian towns, which we may reasonably assume were there in Ponce de Leon's time. Below St. Augustine to Cape Canaveral the Indians inhabited at frequent intervals—a concentration that later led the Spaniards to establish permanent missions for them. Between St. Augustine Inlet and the mouth of the St. Johns was the longest stretch on the upper east coast for which history does not record Indian habitation. It would seem under the circumstances that the only place where Ponce could have landed without the probability of finding evidence of Indians was along this stretch and in the locality where Herrera said he landed. In passing St. Augustine Inlet the vessels were too far out to be seen by the Indians of Seloy (the ancient Indian town found by Menendez on the site of St. Augustine in 1565), and the landfall north of there was likewise far out of their range of vision. The anchorage was much nearer the St. Johns River and at other seasons of the year some roving Indian from those towns might be expected to see the ships, but Laudonniere says this was the season when these Indians were in the interior on their annual hunt "during which time by no means a man can see one Indian."[11]

Evidence conclusive. With all contributing factors in the determination of the question focusing at true latitude 30° 8', there appears to be no reason for doubting the accuracy of Herrera's record that Ponce de Leon came upon the coast of Florida at that point. The next question is the distance he sailed up the coast before anchoring at dark on April 2, where he afterward went ashore and took possession of the country for Spain.

First Landing in Florida

Along the coast line. The coastal trend between St. Augustine Inlet and the mouth of the St. Johns River is generally north-northwest. Ponce approached the coast sailing west-northwest and continued along its length until he anchored. It does not seem possible to construe this clear record of

---

[11] Translation of Laudonniere's account in Virginia Historical Society Early Voyages to America, 1848, p. 444. Laudonniere was the commander of Fort Caroline, the French settlement on the St. Johns six miles above its mouth, 1564-65.

Herrera in any other way than that he continued up the coast toward the mouth of the St. Johns.

Ponce de Leon, running to west-northwest, approached the coast on April 2 in latitude 30° 8'; the water lessening to 9 fathoms at one league from land he ran along the length of coast seeking harbor and at dusk anchored off shore in 8 fathoms of water. Here sometime between April 2 and 8 he went ashore to take possession (first landing). On Friday, the 8th, he made sail in the same direction (up the coast), but soon turned back for the next day he was sailing south a quarter by southeast; he sailed in this direction until April 20, when he saw indications of Indians and anchored (below Cape Canaveral-the second recorded anchorage and the first mention of Indians in Florida).

The landing place. On April 2, at noon, the vessels were three miles off shore half way between St. Augustine Inlet and the mouth of the St. Johns River. They came in closer and continued up the coast until dark, when they anchored. Dusk in this locality at that season of the year comes about half past six. Allowing say thirty minutes for coming in, making soundings and preparing for anchorage (a very reasonable and proper deduction), there were six hours sailing time along the coast to be considered in determining the distance they sailed before anchoring. The speed of the vessels out at sea has already been estimated at two miles an hour, and it is not probable that here along a strange shore their speed would be greater, as Juan Ponce must be credited with being an experienced seaman too cautious to forge full sail ahead under such circumstances. Sailing six hours at two miles an hour therefore indicates a maximum distance along shore of twelve miles. This is as close a determination as can be constructed from Herrera's record. The place of landing can be designated only as a locality—somewhere along the 12-mile length of beach indicated on the foregoing map, with circumstances favoring the upper part of this stretch.

Landing Ceremonies and Activities

Landing ceremonies unknown. Some time between Saturday night, April 2nd, and Friday, the 8th, Ponce de Leon went ashore to view the country and take possession. No mention is made of any ceremony attendant upon the act of taking possession. This omission of details seems to have been accepted by later writers as an invitation to supply them and this has been done in many elaborate interpretations. The scene of taking possession is

The First Landing in Florida

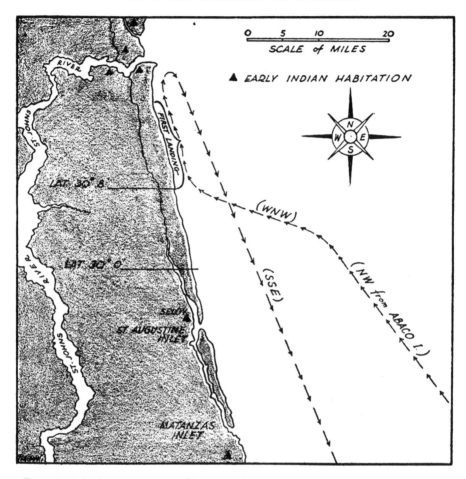

Record of Indian town near Matanzas Inlet is inferential.

Ponce de Leon, running to west-northwest, approached the coast on April 2 in latitude 30° 8'; the water lessening to 9 fathoms at one league from land he ran along the length of coast seeking harbor and at dusk anchored off shore in 8 fathoms of water. Here sometime between April 2 and 8 he went ashore to take possession (first landing). On Friday, the 8th, he made sail in the same direction (up the coast), but soon turned back for the next day he was sailing south a quarter by southeast; he sailed in this direction until April 20, when he saw indications of Indians and anchored (below Cape Canaveral—the second recorded anchorage and the first mention of Indians in Florida).

usually pictured with Ponce surrounded by priests and soldiers kneeling in prayer amidst the banners of church and state, with an audience of interested Indians in the background. Some go so far as to repeat the words used in taking possession, and it has been said that he ended the ceremony with the proclamation that he took possession of the land in the name of Ferdinand and Isabella. Since Isabella had been in her tomb more than eight years, the statement must be wrong. These descriptions may be picturesque, but I can find nothing in the record to support them.

No priests with the expedition. There is no evidence that priests or other ecclesiastics were with the expedition. The patent under which Ponce sailed indicated nothing in this particular, nor does Herrera or any other Spanish historian mention them. The voyage was an expeditionary one and did not necessarily warrant the presence of priests, whose purpose would have been largely to Christianize the Indians. There were situations during the voyage where the presence of a priest aboard would naturally have been indicated had there been one.

Activities unknown. With the exception of the simple statement that Ponce went ashore for information and to take possession, nothing is known historically of what the Spaniards did in the five days they remained at the first anchorage. Any interpretation can be only on the basis of what Ponce's subsequent activities indicate, from which it would appear that he remained in the immediate vicinity of his vessels without any attempt to explore the country. It may be inferred with at least a semblance of backing that the purpose was to await the appearance of Indians (who, however, did not appear), in the meantime making repairs to sails and rigging, which doubtless needed attention as a result of the rough weather through which the vessels had just passed.

Why Named Florida

"Because it had a very beautiful view of many and cool woodlands, and it was level and uniform." The floral decorations usually added originated with Washington Irving, the first American writer upon the subject. Mr. Irving expanded "many and cool woodlands" into "The whole country was in the fresh bloom of spring; the trees were gay with blossoms, and the fields covered with flowers."[12] Woodbury Lowery attempted to identify the flow-

---

[12]   *Voyages and Discoveries of the Companions of Columbus-Ponce de Leon*, Chapter Seven.

ers, though he explained that his list was made up from Bartram's record of the flora of Florida.[13] I have made many visits to that part of the coast around. The first of April and have yet to see more than what Herrera said Ponce de Leon saw. The woodlands were probably much denser then than now, as much of the timber has been cut out for commercial purposes.

"And because, moreover, they discovered it in the time of the feast of flowers [Pascua Florida]." In the *time* of the Feast of Flowers means during the *season* of Easter. Had the discovery been made on Easter Day, March 27th, Herrera unquestionably would have said so in this connection, as that was the most important of all the feast days with the Spaniards. This is further evidence that the land Ponce de Leon saw on Easter Sunday was Abaco Island of the Bahamas as already discussed, and that the discovery of Florida was on Saturday, April 2, 1513, which was yet in the season of Easter as celebrated in that day. Emphasis has been placed on this fact because practically all histories and encyclopedias state that Florida was discovered on Easter Sunday.

Juan Ponce Turns Back

Down the coast line. Leaving his first anchorage Juan Ponce started up the coast, but from a cause unknown and impossible to surmise he sailed only a short distance, then turned back and headed south-southeast parallel to the coast line. In doing so he just missed a most important discovery, for had he sailed a little farther and rounded the south cape of the St. Johns River, he would have seen the river and known from its size that he had discovered the mainland instead of an island as he imagined Florida to be throughout the voyage. The vessels worked their way southward, around Cape Canaveral, where they came in contact with the Gulf Stream. Somewhere below Canaveral Juan Ponce anchored. In this neighborhood he made his second recorded landing in Florida and it was here that he saw the first evidence of Florida Indians.

Biscayne Bay, Florida Keys and Tortugas. Ponce de Leon continued to follow the coast southward, anchoring here and there. He evidently examined Biscayne Bay, for Herrera mentions a bay north of the Florida Keys. He sailed along the entire length of the Florida Keys and on out to the Tortugas, in the vicinity of which he changed course to north.

---

[13] *Spanish Settlements, I,* pp. 138-9.

That Ponce de Leon reached the Tortugas at this time unlocks mysteries that hitherto have been impossible for historians to solve. Describing the voyage Herrera indicates that Juan Ponce was at Biscayne Bay on May 13, and was sailing along the Florida Keys (Martires) on the 15th, "and kept on sailing, sometimes to the north and other times to the northeast." This has been generally taken to mean that he sailed through one of the openings between the Keys and set the north-northeasterly course from there, which would have carried the vessels to the coast east of Cape Sable and not to the west coast at all, a circumstance that could not be reconciled with the text following. The fact that Ponce de Leon "kept on sailing" to the Tortugas before turning north is found in Herrera's statement "On Wednesday [June 15] they went on the lookout for the eleven rocky islets *that they left to the west*. On Thursday and Friday they ran in the same direction until, on Tuesday, the 21st, they reached the rocky islets, *which they named Las Tortugas*." From this we learn that Juan Ponce had passed the Tortugas before and had now returned to them (from a point on the west coast of the Florida peninsula as will be shown presently). This accounts for the "sometimes to the north and other times to the northeast" sailing directions that have always puzzled historians. Passing the Tortugas "to the west" about May 18, Ponce de Leon kept his north course for a time and not finding the Florida mainland, which he had not seen for some days, he turned to northeast, then back to north, and again to northeast, etc., in order to find it, for he knew that Florida had a southern or western coast somewhere.

On the West Coast

Pine Island and Charlotte Harbor. Had Ponce de Leon sailed continuously north from the Tortugas he would have sighted the coast at or near Tampa Bay. Had he taken a straight northeast direction he would have come upon it in the vicinity of Cape Romano. It follows then that under any circumstances the actual contact was within these limits. Let us examine the coast between Tampa Bay and Cape Romano. With Herrera's full description and a modern detailed map of the Florida peninsula before us, it does not require a lengthy study to convince anyone that the only situation corresponding in every way to the description is the region around Charlotte Harbor. Juan Ponce came upon the coast just north of Charlotte Harbor on May 23, and the next day was sailing southerly along the outlying islands, speaking of them as the "islets that extended out into the sea." He found the passage for vessels next to the coast into Carlos Sound and anchored off Pine Island, which he afterward named Matanca, because in a fight with the Indians there several Indians and a Spaniard were killed.[14] In this haven he careened the *San Christoval*—the only vessel of the fleet whose name has been preserved. Later he sent a boat to examine and sound a harbor nearby—Charlotte Harbor.[15] Now back to the sailing directions: The zigzag north and northeast course that Ponce de Leon set would result in an average NNE track and we should look in that general direction from the Tortugas for the landfall. Charlotte Harbor is directly NNE of the Tortugas.

Our examination of the coast located the landfall with reasonable certainty by the description of the locality and the sailing directions now come in to verify it. The evidence is indisputable, and establishes the fact that Ponce de Leon on his voyage of 1513 did not reach a point on the west coast of the Florida peninsula farther north than the 27th parallel; and further, that his activities on that coast on this voyage were confined to the region shown by the accompanying map.

Ponce de Leon leaves Florida. Juan Ponce sailed from Matanca out into the Gulf and headed for the Tortugas. It required nearly a week for him to find them, indicating calms or light airs en route. He named these islands Las Tortugas, because he took in them many turtles, seals (manatee?) and sea birds. From the Tortugas he set a southwesterly course, came upon the extreme western end of Cuba and examined its northern coast for some distance. From Cuba he sailed back along the Florida Reps and on to the Bahamas again.

Exploration of Florida confined to the coast. Nowhere can it be inferred from Herrera's account that Ponce de Leon made any attempt to explore the country away from the immediate coast. His landings everywhere appear to have been for purposes other than exploration, and, after the first landing to take possession, chiefly to get water and firewood for the vessels or to meet the Indians seen on shore, until he came upon the west coast, where at Charlotte Harbor, he seems to have examined the region with a thought of future settlement. The Spaniards associated gold with mountains and as Florida was level and uniform as far as the eye could reach it did not have the

---

14   No other death is mentioned among the Spaniards on the voyage. This man then was the first white man to die in Florida and perhaps in the United States.

15   These early navigators made the same distinction between a bay and a harbor that we do now.

appearance of a gold-producing land. At Charlotte Harbor, however, the Indians had a specimen of guanin, an inferior quality of gold, and Ponce de Leon understood from them that a chief of that neighborhood named Carlos[16] had gold in his possession. It is evident that the implacable fury of the Indians was engendered by every contact with them. Four battles between them and the Spaniards are recorded-two on the lower east coast and two in the Charlotte Harbor region. The cause of the hostility is not explained and must find its solution in the imagination. Students interested in the subject will find in Herrera the first account of the Indians in continental United States, with a description of their weapons and mode of fighting, and enough to form some judgment of their character and habits. They did not fear the white men and only the noise of artillery seemed to frighten them.

Juan Ponce sailed along the Florida Keys and westward as far as the Tortugas, in the neighborhood of which, about May 18, he turned to a "sometimes north and at other times northeast" course that carried him to the west coast of the Florida peninsula on May 23rd. On the 24th he was sailing southerly along a chain of islands "that extended out into the sea" and coming to a passage for vessels between these islands and the coast he entered and anchored off an island inside. In this haven he repaired the San Christoval. He was in the vicinity three weeks and examined and sounded a harbor nearby. On June 15 he sailed out into the Gulf and headed for the Tortugas again. (The upper border of this map represents the 27th parallel of latitude.)

This voyage may be properly divided into a primary and a secondary stage. The primary stage was the hope of discovering new lands with gold mines and Indian slaves to work them, the dream of all of the prominent Spaniards of that day. It was Ponce de Leon's main design. He discovered Florida, followed its coast on the east side and visited the west coast far enough up for him to form the impression that it was a point of land which projected so much that he thought it must be an island. We have followed his track around Florida guided by Herrera's remarkable record and have observed, what must have been true, his hardships and discouragements resulting from failure to find the material things sought or any indication of them. We come now to the other stage of the voyage, the secondary or so-called romantic phase, when Juan Ponce, now in the Bahamas again on his way

---

[16]   This is the first mention of this famous Florida Indian name. It was probably not the real Indian name, but was so interpreted by the Spaniards from the guttural sound of the Indian pronunciation.

At Charlotte Harbor

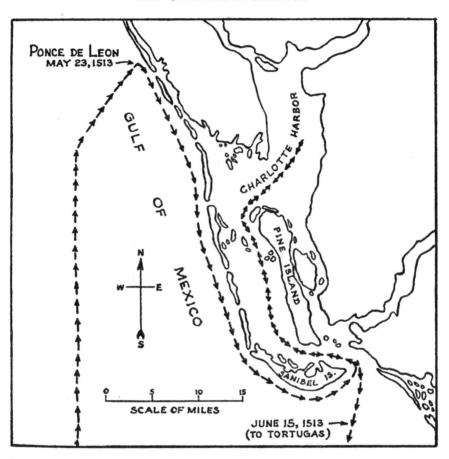

Juan Ponce sailed along the Florida Keys and westward as far as the Tortugas, in the neighborhood of which, about May 18, he turned to a "sometimes north and at other times northeast" course that carried him to the west coast of the Florida peninsula on May 23rd. On the 24th he was sailing southerly along a chain of islands "that extended out into the sea" and coming to a passage for vessels between these islands and the coast he entered and anchored off an island inside. In this haven he repaired the *San Christoval*. He was in the vicinity three weeks and examined and sounded a harbor nearby. On June 15 he sailed out into the Gulf and headed for the Tortugas again. (The upper border of this map represents the 27th parallel of latitude.)

home, starts his search for Bimini as required by his patent and to satisfy himself of the truth or falsity of the Indian tradition about it.

Juan Ponce Searches for Bimini

Among the Bahamas. Upon his return to the Bahamas after leaving Florida, Juan Ponce found an old Indian woman on a lonely island and took her aboard as a guide; her name is not mentioned, though he named the island La Vieja, meaning "old woman." After a while he reached an island that the old woman said was called Bahama. Sailing from island to island in the Bahamas, confused by sea currents that he had not seen in the spring, and afterward beset by storms (hurricane influences probably), Ponce de Leon tired of the quest and sailed for Porto Rico the latter part of September, leaving one of his vessels in the Bahamas to continue the search for Bimini.

Bimini found. In time the vessel left in the Bahamas returned to Porto Rico and reported that Bimini had been found; that it was a large island, well wooded and watered, but contained no spring that "restores old men to youths." Bimini is supposed to have been Andros Island. And says Herrera, "discovery by Juan Ponce of La Florida so ended, without knowledge that it was the mainland; nor for some years thereafter was that assurance obtained."

The Indian Legend

Believed by many, but not by all. The Bimini tradition is the oldest North American legend, as it was in after years that legends of the Vikings in the North began to be considered. It is difficult to determine whether it was really a legend or something manufactured by the Indians to induce the Spaniards to leave. The most complete account of the mythical spring was written by Peter Martyr, probably before the result of Ponce de Leon's voyage became known. Martyr mentions Bimini under another name. His account follows:

> Among the which [the Lucayos or Bahamas] there is an Island, about three hundred and XXV leagues from Hispaniola, as they say which have searched the same, named *Boiuca* or *Agnaneo,* in the which is a continual spring of running water of such marvelous virtue, that the water thereof being drunk, perhaps with some diet,

maketh old men young again. And here must I make protestation to your holiness, not to think this to be said lightly or rashly. For they have so spread this rumor for a truth throughout all the court, that not only all the people, but also many of them whom wisdom or fortune hath divided from the common sort, think it to be true. But if you shall ask my opinion herein, I will answer that I will not attribute so great power to nature, but that God hath no less reserved this prerogative to himself, than to search the hearts of men, or to give substance to privation (that is) being to no being.[17]

The "Fountain of Youth." The nature of this legend kept it alive during the credulous age, but after Ponce de Leon's voyage little attention was paid to it until comparatively modern writers, seeking a romantic theme, revived it and centered it around Juan Ponce like a veil through which the light of history was not allowed to penetrate. And so it has come about that in the popular mind a "fountain of youth" is inseparably associated with the voyage to the exclusion of almost everything else, which elevates it to an importance far greater than it deserves historically.[18] Though the tradition properly belongs to the Bahama Islands, where Bimini was supposed to be, it is now generally applied to Florida. There is no evidence that Ponce de Leon associated Bimini with the land that he discovered on April 2; had he entertained such an idea he would have expressed it at the time of the discovery without bestowing a new name upon the country. The romance of Ponce de Leon's land of Florida is found not in a visionary "fountain of youth," but in its true history of discovery, settlement and subsequent development; in its climate and sunshine, and in its natural and man-made wonders.

Year of Discovery was 1513

It was not until the 1850's that any question was raised concerning the date, 1512, given by Herrera as that of Ponce de Leon's first voyage to Florida. In his researches a German historian, Oscar Peschel, questioned the date and assumed that the voyage was in 1513, because Easter Sunday of that

---

[17] Peter Martyr, *The Decades of the New World or West India*, Second Decade, Tenth Book-Eden's translation. The Second Decade was addressed to "The Bishop of Rome, the tenth of that name" (Pope Leo X).

[18] *See Charles B. Reynolds, The Landing of Ponce de Leon, A Historical Review. 1934.*

year fell on March 27, as recorded by Herrera, and did not in 1512. Sometime in the 1880's this question came up in the general press of the country, I think originally in the *Saturday Evening Post,* and brought on a wide discussion by historians and historical magazines. About the same time Henry Harrisse published his *Discovery of North America*, which advanced Peschel's idea of the 1513 date. The investigation proceeded and Juan Ponce was accounted for during the summer of 1512 as being engaged elsewhere. Finally the numerous dates given in Herrera's account were considered and the week days and feast days mentioned therein were checked with the modern calendar and found to agree in no case with the calendar for 1512, but did agree in every case with the calendar for 1513. This brought on a consideration of old style and new style dates. Though simple in fact, the explanation of the conversion of one calendar to another using a different date to begin the year is a confusing one generally and will be excused here with the statement that the result of the investigation convinced historians and scholars that according to our present system of chronological reckoning the year of the voyage was 1513. This will explain why earlier histories give 1512 as the year of Ponce de Leon's voyage and discovery of Florida, whereas modern historians (subsequently to the 1880's) use the corrected year 1513.

First Florida Names

Given or mentioned by Juan Ponce in 1513. Florida: The oldest European name for any part of the United States. *Punta de Arracifes*: Cape Canaveral. *River La Cruz:* On the lower east coast. *Cape Corrientes:* Extreme eastern part of the coast near Palm Beach. *Abaioa:* Indian village in the neighborhood of Cape Corrientes. *Chequescha:*[19] Biscayne Bay. *Santa Marta* and *Pola:* Islands off Biscayne Bay. *Martires:* Florida Keys. *Achecambei:* One of the Florida Keys, possibly Matecumbe. *Tortugas:* As named now. *Matanca:* Pine Island at Charlotte Harbor. *Carlos:* Indian chief presumably of the Charlotte Harbor-Fort Myers region. *Cautio:* Name for Florida among the Bahama Indians.

---

[19] This, I believe, is the original Indian name for Biscayne Bay, as derived from the circumstances of Ponce de Leon's two visits there in 1513. Fifty years later Menendez called the region Tequesta, and Herrera on his map of 1601 shows it as a coastal indentation called Jequesta.

PONCE DE LEON'S SECOND VOYAGE AND ATTEMPT TO COLONIZE FLORIDA

The Records

Following his voyage of 1513 Ponce de Leon sailed for Spain where he seems to have given a favorable account of his discoveries, for on September 26 (or 27), 1514, the King issued a patent to him to colonize Florida and Beniny, but first required his services against the Caribs, a fierce tribe of Indians inhabiting the Lesser Antilles. Returning to the West Indies Ponce de Leon proceeded against these Indians, but was severely repulsed by them. Mortified at his failure he returned to Porto Rico and remained in semi-retirement several years, apparently giving up the idea of colonizing Florida. In this period several expeditions visited the Florida west coast and one, that of Ayllon, discovered and partially explored what is now the Carolina coast. Juan Ponce was not roused by these more or less predatory expeditions, but when the fame of Cortes in Mexico began to spread through the West Indies he decided to take possession of Florida under the authority of his patent of 1514, issued by King Ferdinand, who had died, the Emperor Charles V being now on the Spanish throne.

This patent is found in *Documentos del Archivo de Indias*, XXII. 33. A translation of this interesting document was published by Dr. L. D. Scisco in *American Catholic Historical Society's Record* for December, 1912. The *Record* has been discontinued and I have been unable to reach Dr. Scisco to ask him for the use of his translation; but anticipating his permission it is used here with full credit to both.

The Patent

The agreement that was made by Our command with you, Juan Ponce de Leon, for the expedition to colonize the island of Beniny and the island of Florida which you discovered by Our command, in addition to the articles and agreement that were made with you when you took action for discovery, is as follows:

First, whereas, in the said articles and agreement made with you by Our command, concerning the discovering and colonizing of the said islands, I gave license and authority, for the time and limitation of three years to commence from the day of delivery to you of the said articles, to conduct at your cost and charge the vessels that you might wish, provided that you stood obligated to begin the expedition of discovery within the first year; and because until now you have occupied yourself in matters of Our service and you have not had time to start the voyage of discovery, it is My will and pleasure that the said three years may commence to run and be reckoned from the day you may embark on your voyage to the said islands.

Item, that as soon as you embark (sic) at the said islands you may summon the chiefs and Indians thereof, by the best device or devices there can be given them, to understand what should be said to them, conformably to a summons that has been drawn up by several learned men, the which will be given to you signed by the Very Reverend Father in Christ, the Bishop of Burgos, Archbishop of Rosario, Our chief chaplain and one of Our council, and by Lope Conchillos, Our secretary and one of Our council and attorneys, by all the ways and means you may be able to devise, that they should come into the knowledge of Our Catholic Faith and should obey and serve as they are bound to do; and you will take down in signed form before two or three notaries, if such there be, and before as many witnesses and these the most creditable, as may be found there, in order that it may serve for Our justification, and you will send the said document; and the summons must be made once, twice, thrice.

And if after the aforesaid they do not wish to obey what is contained in the said summons, you can make war and seize them and carry them away for slaves; but if they do obey, give them the best treatment you can and endeavor, as is stated, by all the means at your disposal, to convert them to Our Holy Catholic Faith; and if by chance, after having once obeyed the said summons, they again rebel, I command that you again make the said summons before making war or doing harm or damage.

Furthermore, whereas in the said articles and agreement that I commanded to be made with you at the time that you were setting forth to discover the said island, I made a grant to the persons who should go to discover the said island of all that might be discovered therein; and that they should pay only a tax of the gold and other metals and things of profit they should find on the islands-the first year a tenth, the second a ninth, the third an eighth, and the fourth a seventh, and the fifth a sixth part, and the other years following a fifth, according to and as it is paid in the island of Espanola; therefore; by these presents I confirm and approve the aforesaid and it is My wish that it shall have effect for the time of the said twelve years, beginning as soon as they begin to colonize the said island.

Furthermore, that I shall give license and I do hereby give it to the said Juan Ponce de Leon to make and build houses in the said island, and villages of habitations of the sort that are made and built in these realms, provided the foundations of such may be with one tapia height of stone and another of earth; and likewise to make whatever provision he sees fit for the raising of corn and grapes and fruit-bearing and non-fruit-bearing trees and whatever other things there may be afforded in the said region.

Item, that, after you may have made war on the said Caribs or protected the chiefs and Indians and brought them peace, you can go or send with the vessels and people of the said expedition to visit the said islands of Beniny and island of Florida, where there may not be need of your presence, and do concerning it what shall seem best for Our service.

Item, for surety that you, the said Juan Ponce, and the members of your expedition are now doing and will fulfill, and that there will be fulfilled, looked after, and paid all that is contained in these articles which it belongs to you to look after and to fulfill, before you make the said voyage (you may give) full and approved guaranties to the satisfaction of Our officials residing in the said island of Santiago [*sic*].[20]

For which, you, the said Juan Ponce, fulfilling all that which is stipulated and each feature and part of it, and having given the said guaranties and looking after and paying the things aforesaid, I promise you and I swear to you by these presents to command and look after and fulfill all that which is contained in these articles and each feature and part of it; and I command Our officials in the island of San Juan that in our name, conformably to the aforesaid, they maintain with you the said agreement and articles and receive the said guaranties; and for your despatch I command Don Diego Colon, Our admiral, viceroy governor of the island of Espanola, and Our judges of appeal there, and Our officials in the said island of San Juan, and all

---

[20]   Should be island of San Juan—Scisco.

the justices, that they give you all favor and aid of which you shall have need, without there being put upon you any hindrance in it or in any manner or part of it.

Done in Valladolid on the twenty-sixth [or twenty-seventh] of September, one thousand, five hundred and [fourteen.]

I, The King

Letters to the Emperor

Juan Ponce de Leon to Charles V. *Documentos ineditos de Indias,* Vol. XL. 50-52:

Porto Rico, February 10, 1521.

Among my services I discovered, at my own cost and charge, the Island Florida, and others in its district, which are not mentioned as being small and useless; and now I return to that island, if it please God's will, to settle it, being enabled to carry a number of people with which I shall be able to do so, that the name of Christ may be praised there, and Your Majesty served with the fruit that land produces. And I also intend to explore the coast of said island further, and see whether it is an island, or whether it connects with the land where Diego Velasquez is, or any other; and I shall endeavor to learn all I can. I shall set out to pursue my voyage hence in five or six days.[21]

De La Gama to His Majesty. *Documentos ineditos de Indias,* Vol. XL. 54:

Porto Rico, February 15, 1521

The Adelantado Juan Ponce de Leon starts from this island [Porto Rico] on the 20th of this month, with another expedition, to settle Florida, and make discoveries in the adjoining country.[22]

---

[21] This translation by Dr. John Gilmary Shea will be found in his "Ancient Florida" in Windsor's *Narrative and Critical History of North America,* Vol. 2, p. 234. "The land where Diego Velasquez is" refers to Mexico.

[22] Translation and reference by Henry Harrisse, *The Discovery of North America,* p. 158.

Authorities on the Voyage

There appears to have been no official report of Ponce de Leon's second voyage to Florida. For information concerning it we must turn to the accounts of the Spanish historians who were in a position to obtain their information first-hand from the survivors of the expedition. Of them only one offers details of the voyage, Gonzalo Fernandez de Oviedo (1478-1557), who was in the West Indies soon after the event collecting material for his history. His account was contemporaneous and though a "memory" record it has every appearance of being reasonable and authentic. His original manuscript was not published in full until the 1850's. Herrera, whose main dependence was official documentary evidence, did not give an extended account of this voyage; his record is contained in a summarized farewell to Ponce de Leon and is evidently based in part on Oviedo's account.

Other Spanish historians of the 16th century, namely, Las Casas, Gomara, Torquemada, Garcilaso, and later Barcia, mentioned the voyage, but their accounts are extremely brief, often confused, and add nothing new to the subject. For these reasons they are not included here, except an item from Garcilaso.

The translations of the Oviedo and Herrera records herein were rendered for and contributed to this work by Dr. C. L. Crow, Head of the Department of Spanish, University of Florida. These scholarly translations by Dr. Crow make available to students of Florida's history valuable historical information which has hitherto remained generally unknown to them.

OVIEDO, *Historia General y Natural de las Indias* . . . Madrid, 1853, Vol. 2, Part 2, Book 36, Chapter 1, pp. 622-623:

> . . . not exhausted by his outlays and labors, he [Johan Ponce] fitted out anew with more care and at greater expense, and equipt and put in order certain ships,[23] so as to reach along the Mainland on the shores lying to the North, that coast and point which projects into the

---

[23] There were two main ships: Juan Ponce to Adriano-Harrisse, *Discovery of North America,* p. 158; Wm. R. Shepherd, *Guide to Materials for the History of the United States in Spanish Archives, p.* 68 (July 4, 1523); Herrera, Torquemada, Barcia.

sea about a hundred leagues in length and fifty in breadth. And it seemed to him that in addition to what could be learned and known of the islands which are to be found there, also on the Mainland could be learned other secrets and important things, and [that] those peoples could be converted to God to the great profit of himself in particular and in general for all those who were accompanying him, for, as has been said, two hundred men and fifty horses were in the ships. And before placing this fleet in readiness, he spent much: and passed over to that land during the month of . . . of the year one thousand and five hundred and twenty:[24] and as a good colonist, he took mares and heifers and swine and sheep and goats and all kinds of domestic animals (and) useful in the service of mankind: and also for the cultivation and tillage of the field[s] he was supplied with all [kinds of] seed, as if the business of colonization consisted of nothing more than to arrive and cultivate the land and pasture his livestock. But the temperature of the region was very unsuitable and different from what he had imagined, and the natives of the land [were] a very austere and very savage and belligerous and fierce and untamed people and not accustomed to a peaceful existence nor to lay down their liberty so easily at the discretion or alien volition of other men, nor at the determination of those monks and priests by whom he was accompanied for the exercise of religious rites and the service of the church, nor even though they preached as much as they wished, could they be understood in as short a time as was imagined by them and by him who led them there, if God with his absolute power did not cause them to be understood by those very barbarous peoples and idolatrous savages (and) laden with sins and vices. I mean, that altho, as in truth all which seems difficult is easy for God to do, when it pleases him, it is well for us to reflect that we are not deserving of that facility, nor are those trout caught with so little effort: and he desires first the reformation of the fishermen, so that those who are to hear and follow them may come to a knowledge of the truth. Notwithstanding that with this captain went religious persons and [ones] of sound doctrine; but inasmuch as everything went wrong, and the fleet was lost[25] and the captain and the season and plantation jointly

---

[24] This is obviously a "memory" error in the year; the deletion of the month is in the original text.

and within a few days, it is to be believed that God was not served nor the time come for the conversion of that land and province to our holy Catholic faith, since he permits the devil still to keep those Indians deceived and for his own, and the population of hell to be augmented with their souls.

This fleet arrived at that land in the year that has been mentioned: and then the adelantado Johan Ponce, when he disembarked, gave order, as a prudent man, that his men should rest: and when it seemed to him proper, he moved forward with his retinue and attacked by land and entered into a skirmish or battle with the Indians, as he was a valiant captain and was among the first, and not so adroit [in battle] in that land as on the islands, so many and such of the enemy charged, that his men and his courage did not suffice to withstand them. And finally they defeated him and killed a number of the Christians, and more than twice as many Indians died, and he escaped wounded grievously by an arrow; and he decided to go to the island of Cuba to be cured, if it were possible, and with a greater retinue and more strength to return to this conquest. And so he embarked and arrived at the island [and] at the port of Havana, where after he had arrived, he lived a short time: but he died as a Catholic and after having received the sacraments, and also died others who were wounded, and others of illnesses.

HERRERA, *Historia General de los Hechos. . . .*, 1601, Decade 3, Book 1, Chap. 14, pp. 30-31:

The reputation of Hernando Cortes kept spreading and his fame gaining more repute, which aroused the ambition of many of the foremost senior captains of the Indies to undertake deeds of daring; because they, being of the generation of Hernando Cortes, considered themselves as no less [worthy]. One of these was Governor General Juan Ponce de Leon, who from the year twelve, when he discovered Florida, and went seeking that sacred fountain, so renowned among the Indians, and the river, whose waters rejuve-

---

[25]   Evidently after the arrival of the ship at Havana. It is said that one of the vessels made port at Vera Cruz, Mexico, but there are reasons for doubting the accuracy of this. (Read in connection with text paragraph following.)

nated the aged: and after the Caribs of the island of Guadalupe treated him ill, had remained in retirement. Now he determined to fit out on the island of San Juan de Puerto-Rico, where he had his residence, two ships, on which he spent a large part of his fortune; went with them to Florida, which was still considered an island, in order to satisfy himself in passing, as to whether it was mainland, as he says in his letters, which he wrote this year[26] to the Emperor, to Cardinal Adriano, governor of these realms, at that time, and to Secretary Samano. And when he had set foot on land in Florida, after having suffered many hardships during the voyage, the Indians sallied out to oppose him, and fighting stubbornly against him, killed some of his men, and he, wounded in a thigh, returned, with the survivors, to Cuba, where he ended his days, and the King, in consideration of his services, gave his jurisdiction, and the other concessions which he held, to his son, Luis Ponce de Leon.

GARCILASO DE LA VEGA, *La Florida del Inca*, Madrid, 1723, Book 6, Chapter 22, page 266:

Text decidedly confused but from which may be gathered that in the battle with the Indians at the time of the attempted settlement not less than eighty of Ponce de Leon's men were killed or died of their wounds. [This indicates either an ambuscade or an overwhelming force of Indians.]

Review

Place of the attempted settlement. The clue to the coast of Florida on which Ponce de Leon attempted to plant his colony is found in his letter to Charles V: "And I intend to explore the coast of said island further, and see . . . whether it connects with the land where Diego Velasquez is. . . ." Juan Ponce had ranged the east coast of Florida throughout its length on his first voyage and it is evident that on this, second voyage, he intended to follow the coast line westward to Mexico, where Velasquez at the time was involved. For this purpose he would naturally select a place on the west coast to plant

---

[26] The year is not stated in the text, but is given in a running head at the top of the page as 1521.

his settlement and proceed from there to examine the coast westward. Now where on the west coast did he attempt to plant his colony?

Referring to the first voyage it was proven that the only place visited by Ponce de Leon on the west coast was the Charlotte Harbor region. He remained there three weeks and examined the locality and its harbor, apparently with the thought of future settlement. There was the only place where he heard of gold in Florida among the Indians—a lure at which these early Spaniards never failed to bite, and a circumstance having a bearing on the question in hand. We know today—and the natural situation has not changed since Ponce de Leon's time—that the locality furnishes everything that could be required for a place of settlement such as he contemplated. With a situation fulfilling all requirements already known to him, is it reasonable to suppose that Juan Ponce, having a cargo a part of which required prompt landing, would spend time unnecessarily in looking for another location? And finally after he landed we see a strong similarity in the conduct of the Indians with that experienced by him with the Carlos Indians at Charlotte Harbor on the first voyage. Oviedo's statement that Juan Ponce experienced a temperature different from that expected can be reconciled to the Charlotte Harbor section, for in the cool waves of early spring it is not unusual for the temperature to fall into the 40's Fahrenheit, which to one acclimated to the West Indies would be considered very cold—there were no thermometers in that day to determine the actual temperature.

The direct evidence furnished by these records is not sufficient to permit the positive statement that Juan Ponce on his second voyage to Florida attempted to plant his colony at Charlotte Harbor; but it can be said that all inferences point that way.

Firsts of History

This voyage produced a number of "firsts" of history for the North American continent: The first attempt to plant a bona-fide self-sustaining colony; the first effort to implant the Christian religion among the Indians;[27] the first monks and priests assigned for permanent residence; and the first purposed agricultural, horticultural, and stock-raising enterprise.

---

[27]   Mexico excluded. Cortes was in Mexico at this time, but that expedition was one of exploration that developed into a military conquest which was still in progress; however, there were two ecclesiastics with the expedition.

PONCE DE LEON CHRONOLOGY

The First Voyage, 1513

March 3: Embarked from Porto Rico.

March 14: Arrived at San Salvador, Bahamas.

March 27 (Easter Sunday): Passed Abaco Island, Bahamas, sailing north-west.

April 2 (Saturday): Discovered Florida in latitude 30° 8'. (Approximately 18 miles south of mouth of St. Johns River.)

April 2-8: Between these dates landed and took possession. (Somewhere on the 12-mile stretch of beach north of 30° 8'.)

April 9: Sailed south-southeasterly following coast line.

April 20: Anchored off Indian town below Cape Canaveral.

May 8: Off Palm Beach (Cape Corrientes).

May 13: At Biscayne Bay (Chequescha).

May 15: Along the Florida Keys (The Martires).

May 18: Passed The Tortugas, sailing northerly.

May 23: Reached the west coast near Charlotte Harbor.

May 24-June 15: At Charlotte Harbor and immediate vicinity.

June 21-24: At The Tortugas again.

June 26-July 1: Along the northern coast of Cuba.

July 3: Along Florida Keys-to Biscayne Bay (Chequescha).

July 18: At La Vieja (Old Woman's I.), Bahamas.

July 25-September 27: Among Bahamas in quest of Bimini.

September 28c: Sailed for Porto Rico.

October 19c: Arrived at Porto Rico.

The Second Voyage

February 20, 1521:[28] Embarked from Porto Rico for Florida. This is the only
date indicated in the records of the second voyage. Ponce de Leon's death
apparently was in the following May or June.

---

[28]   Date as mentioned in the De la Gama letter, page 57. Whether the year corresponds to 1522
when considered in relation to our modern calendar depends upon the date from which the
year was reckoned by the Spanish calendar at the time-a question that I have not been able to
determine with historical certainty.

The Exploration of Florida and Sources on the Founding of St. Augustine

Luis Rafael Arana

July - October 1965

I

Four hundred years ago, Europeans made the first permanent settlement within the present limits of the United States. These were Spaniards who under Pedro Menéndez de Avilés established St. Augustine in 1565, upon land discovered fifty-two years earlier. In the interval between discovery and colonization, the coast of Florida had been gradually charted and portions of the interior explored. Though all attempts at planting the civilization of Spain in the new land failed until Menéndez appeared on the scene, the discoveries of Juan Ponce de León, Alonso Alvarez de Pineda, Pánfilo de Narváez, and Hernando de Soto gradually outlined the contour of the peninsula, brought it within the known lands of the world, and contributed to the eventual success of Menéndez. This paper summarizes the accomplishments of those explorers and furnishes translations of the four contemporary accounts of the founding of St. Augustine.

Ponce de León

In seeking new lands, Juan Ponce de León wanted compensation for the loss of the Puerto Rico governorship. His appointment by King Fernando had violated the prerogatives of the Colón family, as the Council of Castilla so ruled in 1511. The king, however, hoped that Ponce would discover and settle one of several islands rumored to be near Puerto Rico. Because of the stories told by the Indians, the former governor chose Bimini and remitted a proposal for colonization.[1] King Fernando drafted a patent, February 23, 1512, for the discovery and settlement which he hoped thirty-eight year old Ponce would accept.[2] According to his patent, Ponce would pay for the expenses of the expedition be the governor and *adelantado* of Bimini and of any other lands he might discover, and exploit the wealth of the island. The

---

[1] Vincente Murga Sanz, *Juan Ponce de León* (San Juan, 1959), 73, 77-78, 99.

king reserved for himself the construction and control of fortifications and the distribution of Indians. To spur Ponce on, Fernando remarked that Bartolomé Colón would surely accept that task with less advantageous terms.[3]

Ponce de León would not have discovered Florida had he not accepted the Bimini patent promptly and arranged for the voyage. On December 10 the king informed the royal officials of La Espanola that Ponce was really needed in Puerto Rico, and he ordered them to cease negotiations with him and to bestow the patent on some one less interested in profit. Ponce, however, had already gone to La Española, had accepted the royal terms, and had fitted out two vessels, *Santa Maria de la Consolación* and *Santiago,* for the voyage. He registered his ships on January 29, 1513, and quickly sailed for Puerto Rico where he added the *San Cristóbal* to the expedition.[4] The *Santa María* carried forty-one passengers including Ponce, and the *Santiago* had twenty-six persons aboard.[5] Ponce was ready to sail before the king's change of mind became generally known.

The search for Bimini resulted in the discovery of Florida. Ponce departed from the Puerto Rican coast the night of March 4, and on Easter Sunday, March 27, he sighted an island (Abaco) which he did not recognize. A few days later, on April 2, the ships approached the Florida coast, sighting land at 30° 8' north latitude. Coasting northward, he anchored at nightfall. Within the next five days, Ponce landed and took possession of the territory in the name of his king. He named it Florida since it provided a very beauti-

---

[2]   Ponce de León stated in September 1514, during the proceedings held in Valladolid to make him formally the adelantado of Florida, that he was forty years old. *Ibid.,* 118. If so, he was thirty-eight at the time of his drafting of the patent to discover and settle Bimini, and thirty-nine when he discovered Florida.

[3]   *Ibid.,* 100-02; transcript from the original manuscript in *Collections de documentos inéditos relativos al descubrimiento, conquista y colonización de las antiguas posesiones españolas en América y Oceanía,* 42 vols. (Madrid, 1864-1884), XXII, 26-32, and Aurelio Tió, *Nuevas fuentes para la historia de Puerto Rico* (San German, Puerto Rico, 1961), 476-80; English translation in Woodbury Lowery, *The Spanish Settlements within the Present Limits of the United States, 1513-1561* (New York, 1959), 437-41. Lowery (p. 135) as well as Herbert E. Bolton, *The Spanish Borderlands* (New Haven, 1921), 6, erroneously state that the 1512 patent was granted by Charles V. Charles did not become king of Aragon until January 1516, and of Castilla until April 1516. Rafael Altamira, *Manual de historia de España,* 2d ed. (Buenos Aires, 1946), 311-12, 315, 341-43.

[4]   Murga, *Juan Ponce de León,* 103-106.

[5]   *Ibid.,* photographs of the registers covering the *Santiago* and the *Santa María de la Consolación,* facing 102, 104, 106, 108, 110, 112.

ful view of many cool woodlands, it was level and uniform, and it had been discovered on *Pascua Florida,* the feast of the flowers.[6]

On April 8 Ponce ordered the ships north again, but the following day he reversed his course and moved in a southeasterly direction down the coast of Florida. Passing the Cabo de los Arrecifes (Cape Kennedy), he met, on April 21, the full force of the Gulf Stream; then he put into Río de la Cruz (Jupiter Inlet), where he made a stone cross and inscribed it. On May 8 he sailed past Cabo de Las Corrientes (Lake Worth Inlet), the easternmost bend of the coast, and until May 16 followed a course parallel to Los Mártires, Ponce's name for the Florida Keys. The expedition then turned north northeast reaching a point on the lower Gulf coast above Charlotte Harbor on May 23. Then, coasting southward, Ponce stopped at two islands which stood out to sea (Sanibel and Captiva). Remaining in the area until June 14, he explored a harbor (Charlotte), watered his vessels, and traded and fought with the Indians. Many natives were killed on Matanza Island (Pine Island). On June 15 Ponce sailed southwestward and six days later reached Tortugas which he named.[7]

Unlike Florida, Bimini was discovered by someone other than Ponce de León. From the Tortugas, his ships coasted along northwest Cuba, searching for Bimini, but the journey among the Bahama Islands became so protracted that Ponce probably worried that others might report and lay claims to his own discoveries. Consequently, on September 17, he detached Captain Juan Pérez Ortubia with the *San Cristóbal* and ordered him to keep searching. The next day he set his own course for Puerto Rico, arriving there twenty-one days later. On February 20, 1514, Captain Pérez appeared, announcing the discovery of Bimini which he described as a large cool island with many springs and woodlands, but no gold or silver was found.[8]

---

[6] *Ibid.,* 107-08; Tió, *Nuevas fuentes,* 333, 552-53, 558, 559-62, 564-66, 579; T. Frederick Davis, "History of Juan Ponce de León's Voyages to Florida," *Florida Historical Quarterly,* XIV (July 1935), 16-17, 38-39.

[7] Murga, *Juan Ponce de León,* 108-12; Tió, *Nuevas fuentes,* 333-34, 553; Davis, "Ponce de León's Voyages to Florida," 17-21. Lowery, *Spanish Settlements,* 141, and Bolton, *Spanish Borderlands,* 8, confuse Cabo de las Corrientes with Cape Kennedy. Edward W. Lawson, *The Discovery of Florida and its Discoverer Juan Ponce de León* (St. Augustine, 1946), feels that the cabo is Jupiter Light, north of Lake Worth Inlet (p. 38); that the vicinity of Sanibel was the northern limit of Ponce's exploration on the southwest coast (p. 40), and thus the harbor explored is San Carlos Bay rather than Charlotte; and that Matanza is Estero, rather than Pine Island (p. 41).

The legend about a fountain of youth seemed to have been connected with Ponce de León in Spain rather than in America. He and Pérez reported in person their finds and discoveries to King Fernando in April 1514, but they could display no treasure or rare and valuable finds such as had come from the West Indian islands. Perhaps it was Pérez who talked about the Indian legend, and in jest the Court said that Ponce had indeed gone searching for a fountain that guaranteed perpetual youth rather than mundane things like gold or precious gems. Whoever was the author of the report, it is true that as early as December 1514, Peter Martyr, the historian, was writing the Pope about the rumored existence in the New World of a spring whose water rejuvenated old men. Martyr, however, did not attempt to link or connect this story to Ponce de León.[9] It was the historian Gonzalo Fernández de Oviedo, who in 1535, originated the story that Ponce had wasted time searching for the fountain of youth during his voyage.[10] Escalante de Fontaneda,[11] survivor of the Florida shipwreck, exaggerated the legend so much in his report in 1575, that the historian Antonio de Herrera, in 1601, regarded the search for the fabulous spring as important as the true objective of Ponce's expedition.[12] Contemporary manuscripts so far uncovered do not mention the fountain of youth nor indicate that Ponce de León was even aware of the fantasy.[13] Certainly if he had believed the Indian legend, he would hardly have delegated the search for Bimini, reputedly the location of the fountain, to another captain. He would certainly have saved such a great prize for himself.

---

[8]   Murga, *Juan Ponce de León,* 112-14; Davis, "Ponce de León's Voyages to Florida," 22-23.

[9]   Murga, *Juan Ponce de León,* 114-15, 118-20.

[10]   *Memoria de las cosas y costa y indios de la Florida, que ninguno de cuantos la han costeado, no lo han sabido declarar,* "Colección Munoz" (Real Academia de la Historia), LXXXIX; *Colección de documentos inéditos,* V, 532-46; translated into French as "Mémoire sur la Floride," H. Ternaux-Compans, *Recueil de pieces sur la Floride* (Paris, 1841), 9-37; English translations in Buckingham Smith, *Letter of Hernando de Soto and Memoir of Hernando de Escalante Fontaneda* (Washington, 1854), 11-26; B. F. French, *Historical Collections of Louisiana and Florida,* 2d series (New York, 1875), 235-65; and David O True, *Memoir of Dº d'Escalante Fontaneda respecting Florida* (Coral Gables, 1945).

[11]   *Historia general y natural de las Indias, islas y tierra firme del Mar Océano* (Sevilla, 1535), libro XVI, cap. II, in *ibid.,* 119.

[12]   *Historia general de los hechos de los castellanos en las islas y tierra firme del Mar Océano* (Madrid, 1601), década Iª, libro IX, cap. XII, in Murga, *Juan Ponce de León,* 127, note 37.

[13]   Murga, *Juan Ponce de León,* 119.

Alvarez de Pineda

It was impossible to tell from Ponce de León's discovery very much about the geography of Florida. The next exploration there charted the rest of the Gulf coast and determined that the land was not an island but a peninsula. Antón de Alaminos, Ponce's former pilot, had first suggested the need to search for a passage dividing the mainland, and in 1519, Alonso Alvarez de Pineda, commanding four vessels belonging to Francisco de Garay, governor of Jamaica, took up the quest. Pineda first struck the north shore of the Gulf of Mexico at a yet unknown location, and then coasted east and southward along the west shore of Florida. He found he could not maneuver the south end of Florida because of adverse winds and the power of the Gulf Stream. He was forced to retrace his course, noting rivers and bays along the bay. From time to time he landed and took possession at various points, marking the limits of his discovery as he traveled. Alvarez coasted all the way to Panuco (Tampico) and then circled back. While Alvarez discovered the mouth of a large river, supposedly the Mississippi, he found no strait during his nearly nine-month cruise, indicating that Florida was part of a large land mass.[14]

Pánfilo de Narváez

With the general shape of Florida's shore line thus delineated, penetration into the interior became the special achievement of still another Spanish explorer, Pánfilo de Narváez. On December 11, 1526, he obtained a patent authorizing him to conquer, settle, and govern the mainland between Río de las Palmas (near Tampico) and the Cape of Florida.[15] Narváez sailed from Jagua (Cuba) on February 20, 1528, and nearly two months later, on April 16, he reached Bahía de la Cruz (the mouth of Johns Pass, west of Pinellas peninsula) on the Gulf coast of Florida. Taking possession of the area two days later, he then probed northeast from his landing point and discovered a large bay (Old Tampa Bay) which swept inland and two Indian villages (Safety Harbor and Tampa).[16]

---

[14] Lowery, *Spanish Settlements,* 149-51.

[15] *Ibid.,* 173.

[16] *Final Report of the United States De Soto Expedition Commission* (Washington, 1939), 109-13. Cited hereafter as *Final Report.*

On a twentieth century Florida map, Narváez explored the area from Tampa Bay to Wakulla County. The Spanish moved out on May 2, and quickly reached the Withlacoochee River, which they explored to the sea and found its mouth to be a shallow inlet with no harbor. Striking out northward on May 23, Narváez and his men traversed the uninhabited country west of what is now Gainesville, apparently missing the Indians living in that section. North of the Santa Fe River, Narváez turned toward the west, and on June 18 he crossed the Suwannee River between present-day Dowling Park and Ellaville. Moving across the Aucilla River between Lamont and Aucilla, he reached Ivitachuco village on June 25. Narváez resumed the march on July 20 and eight days later, having traveled in a southwesterly direction, he arrived at the mound near Wakulla Springs. On August 3 Narváez turned south, reaching the Gulf coast, perhaps near Piney Island.[17]

This first venture into Florida's interior ended with tragedy at sea. In the seven long weeks spent on the coast, the dispirited men having despaired of being rescued, used the crude tools at hand to construct five makeshift boats. On September 22 the party pushed out into the Gulf; their plan was to sail west until they reached Panuco, a fairly short distance away, they believed. One after the other the boats were lost and men died from drowning and exposure. Narváez was himself blown out to sea and never seen again. Only four survivors, including Alvar Núñez Cabeza de Vaca, eventually struggled back to civilization to report on their harrowing experiences.[18]

Narváez' vessels had been moving up and down the Gulf coast of Florida while he was exploring the interior. The ships first sailed northward from Bahía de la Cruz. Then, reversing course, they moved south about five leagues and discovered Tampa Bay, which had already been seen by land reconnaissance. Then, for many months the fleet tried unsuccessfully to find Narváez and ultimately the vessels proceeded to México.[19]

Hernando de Soto

A patent was bestowed on Hernando de Soto, April 20, 1537, permitting him to conquer, pacify, and settle all the lands that had been under the jurisdiction of Pánfilo de Narváez and Lucas Vázquez de Ayllón. He would

---

17   *Ibid.,* 113-16.
18   Bolton, *Spanish Borderlands,* 23-25, 36-37.
19   *Final Report,* 112.

finance the enterprise and lead it in person. As governor and captain general, *adelantado,* and high constable over 200 leagues of coast designated by him within the territorial concession, he would have power to "distribute Indians." The patent permitted de Soto to select for himself twelve leagues square of land, provided the tract included neither seaport nor principal town. He controlled the fortifications which he would build at his expense. To secure the necessary logistical support for his enterprise, de Soto was also made governor of Cuba.[20] Thus began a new expedition to Florida, the most extended exploration of the vast area that now makes up the southeastern part of the United States.

De Soto departed from Havana on May 18, 1539, and several days later he anchored outside Bahía del Espíritu Santo on the west coast of Florida. Having completed a hazardous passage through the channel into port, the army landed on a beach. Then, concentrating his men in a village on a nearby island, de Soto took possession in the name of his country on June 3. Later, he moved the camp to another village and sent an advance party inland. The *bahía* today is the south shore of Tampa Bay, and the channel is either Passage Key Inlet or Southwest Channel. Terra Ceia Bay is the port that he reached, and Shaw's Point was the landing beach. The island where the army first grouped was Terra Ceia.[21]

De Soto began the first phase of his exploration on July 15, after leaving a base and the small vessels at Terra Ceia Bay. De Soto reached Luca (between Dade City and Istachatta), where the advance party joined him on July 21. He then followed the west side of a league-wide swamp (Tsala Apopka Lake), and after crossing the Withlacoochee River in the vicinity of Stokes Ferry, veered northeastward. On July 29 de Soto entered the deserted capital of Ocale Province, located on the stream below present day Silver Springs.[22]

---

20   *Ibid.,* 76-79.

21   *Ibid.,* 118-39. The location of de Soto's campsite at the village on Terra Ceia Island has been challenged by Ripley P. Bullen, *The Terra Ceia Site, Manatee County, Florida, Florida Anthropological Society Publications,* No. 3 (Gainesville, 1951), and "De Soto's Ucita and the Terra Ceia Site," *Florida Historical Quarterly,* XXX (April 1952), 317-23. The identification of the bay as Tampa Bay, and the entire de Soto route through Florida, has been challenged by Warren H. Wilkinson, *Opening the Case Against the U. S. De Soto Commission's Report* (Jacksonville Beach, 1960). At least two points raised by Wilkinson, the distances travelled daily and the meaning of the terms *ancón* and *decaídos,* indicate that de Soto's travel through Florida should be reinvestigated.

22   *Final Report,* 141-44, 148-52.

Departing from Ocale on August 11, de Soto moved out to the northwest, passing west of Orange Lake and through the narrow land between Levy and Alachua lakes. He then veered north at Alachua village, crossed the Santa Fe River between the mouths of Olustee Creek and New River, and reached Caliquen village (between the creek and the Santa Fe) on August 18. Moving out again on September 9, he took a northwest course, crossed Olustee Creek, and turned west after passing near present day Lake City. He reached Napituca village (near either Houston or Live Oak) on September 15. Eight days later, the Spanish continued their trek, crossing the Suwanee near Dowling Park, then on through the Lake Sampala area and Agile village, until they reached the Aucilla River which they crossed at a point between Lamont and Aucilla on October 3. Ivitachuco, the first Apalachee village they reached, was deserted, but de Soto ordered his force forward. They passed close to Mill Creek, and on October 6 they reached the empty Tallahassee area. Here de Soto decided to establish camp and spend the winter.[23]

There was some minor exploration in Apalachee due to the change of base from Tampa Bay to Apalachee Bay: to the south of the camp, Wakulla Spring, and the coast back of Piney Island where Narvaez had built the boats a few years before. From the new Apalachee base site, Francisco Maldonado, during December and January, explored the Gulf coast to the west and discovered Bahia de Ochuse (probably Pensacola). De Soto closed the new base by dispatching the vessels to Havana, and was then ready to embark upon his travels through Georgia, South and North Carolina, Tennessee, Alabama, Mississippi, Arkansas, Louisiana, and Texas. This part of the exploring journey began on March 3, 1540, when de Soto broke camp and ordered his force northward from Tallahassee.[24]

The Florida exploration between 1513 and 1565 had many results. The east and southwest coasts and keys of Florida were first discovered by Ponce de León. Then in 1519, Alvarez de Pineda located and established the fact that this was a peninsula of the mainland. Thus, within six years after discovery, Florida was fully charted on the maps of the world. The interior remained *terra incognita* until 1528, when Narváez opened the region between Pinellas peninsula and Wakulla County and his vessels moved into Tampa Bay. The interior frontier of this region was extensively enlarged when de Soto entered Florida in 1539. No less important, de Soto's vessels followed a por-

---

[23]   *Ibid.,* 144-48, 152-60.
[24]   *Ibid.,* 161-66.

tion of Alvarez de Pineda's twenty-year old track and discovered Pensacola Bay. While Ponce, Narváez, and de Soto failed in the colonizing required by their patents, in little more than twenty-five years their explorations expanded geographical knowledge of Florida.

II

There are four contemporary Spanish accounts of the founding of St. Augustine by Pedro Menéndez de Avilés. These include a letter written by Menéndez himself, a narrative of the events in Florida by Francisco López de Mendoza Grajales, an unfinished biography of Menéndez by Gonzalo Solís de Merás, and another biography by Bartolomé Barrientos.[25]

Menéndez's Letter

The letter was the first source recorded. Dated September 11, 1565, it was the second communication that Menéndez wrote from Florida to the crown. In it, he reported the landfall, the encounter with the French at the mouth of the St. Johns, the establishment of St. Augustine at Matanzas Bay, his prospective plan of operations, the disposition of the galLeón unable to enter the bay, the need for logistical support from Puerto Rico, Santo Domingo, and Havana, the organization of his army, and the fact that the Indians living south of St. Augustine had some gold of varying quality.[26]

---

[25] A "Relación del suceso de la Florida," Archivo General de Indias, Audiencia of Santo Domingo, legajo 231, 7 folios, (cited hereafter as AGI, Santo Domingo), may be regarded as a fifth contemporary source. This is an account compiled from letters written by Menéndez to the crown dated September 10, October 15, and December 5 and 12, 1565. It is in draft form, penned by an official for revision by the king, and seemingly intended as a memorandum for the files. The draft bears the notation, "Well done, and clean copy can be made." The "Relación" talks about Menéndez's departure from Havana, the arrival in Florida, the encounter with the French at the mouth of the St. Johns, Ribault's move against St. Augustine, the surprise of Fort Caroline, the first massacre at Matanzas, and the Spanish construction of outposts for protection of the Caroline area. The death of Ribault which was already known, is not mentioned because Menéndez had advised that it would be better if that fact became known in France much later. The "Relación" is confusing in regard to the chronology of the events, and does not add to the data in the other contemporary sources about the founding of St. Augustine. The "Relación" is on microfilm at Castillo de San Marcos National Monument, St. Augustine.161-66.

[26] AGI, Santo Domingo, 6 folios.

The letter, together with six others written by Menéndez about the Florida enterprise, became available in the United States through the efforts of Buckingham Smith who furnished copies to Francis Parkman. They were translated into English by Henry Ware in 1870, and were printed by the Massachusetts Historical Society in 1894.[27] Meanwhile in Spain, the original letters and a vast amount of other Menéndez material, had been published in 1893 by Eugenio Ruidíaz y Caravia.[28]

This writer's English translation of the part of the September 11 letter which deals with the founding of St. Augustine has been made from a microfilm of the original:

> . . . I resolved to come toward the Bahama Channel in search of a port where I could land near them [the French]; and eight leagues by sea from their port, and six by land, I found one, which is scarcely thirty degrees and a half, which I had reconnoitered previously on the day of St. Augustine. On the sixth of this month, I disembarked two hundred soldiers there, and on the seventh, three small ships came in with another three hundred and the married men with their wives and children, and I landed most of the artillery and munitions that I was bringing. On the eighth, the day of Our Lady, as another hundred persons, some artillery and munitions, and many provisions which had to be disembarked, were being landed, the French flagship and the admiral's ship came within half a league of us, showing combat signals and maneuvering about us. Remaining at anchor, we signalled them to board us. At three o'clock in the afternoon, they spread sail and went away to their port; and I went ashore and took possession in the name of Your Majesty, and the captains and the officials swore fealty to me as governor and captain general and adelantado of this land and coast, according to the instructions from Your Majesty. Many Indians were present, and among them, many leaders. They appear to be our friends, and it seems to us that they are hostile toward the French . . .

> With the first two hundred soldiers, I sent two captains ashore, who were Juan de San Vicente, brother of Captain San Vicente, and

---

27 *Proceedings of the Massachusetts Historical Society,* 2d series (Boston, 1894), VIII, 415-68.
28 Eugenio Ruidíaz y Caravia, *La Florida: su conquista y colonización por Pedro Menéndez de Avilés,* 2 vols. (Madrid, 1893), II, 74-84.

Andrés López Patiño, veteran soldiers, to dig a trench at the most suitable site, at which place the people who would land could gather together and fortify themselves for defense, should the enemy come upon them. They [the captains] did it so well that when I landed, on the day of Our Lady, to take possession of the land in the name of Your Majesty, it seemed as though they had had a month's time. They could not have done better with shovels, pick mattocks, and iron tools, although we do not have any of these materials, because the ship bringing them has not arrived. I bring blacksmiths and iron to have these tools made in little time, and I shall do so. As I have landed, we will inspect the site which seems to us most suitable to fortify, because where we are is not suitable. It will be well for us to do this as soon as possible before the enemy finds us. If they give us eight days' time, it seems to us we will accomplish [this objective]. . .
29

Narrative of Father López

The narrative written by Father Francisco López de Mendoza Grajales about the events connected with the establishment of Florida covers the period from the Cádiz sailing to the end of the first massacre at Matanzas. López, chaplain of the expedition, penned the account shortly after the latter event. Three copies of the narrative in Spanish are found in different manuscript collections.[30] A French translation by H. Ternaux-Compans was published in Paris in 1841;[31] the document was published in Spain in 1865;[32] and an English translation by B. F. French was published in 1875.[33] Ruidíaz published it in Spanish again, together with other Menéndez material, in 1893.[34] The English translation by French has been reprinted singly.[35]

---

29 AGI, Santo Domingo, folios 3, 4-5.

30 "Colección Munoz" (RAH), LXXXVII: "Colección Navarrete" (Deposito Hidrografico), XIV; Buckingham Smith Collection (New York Public Library), vol. for 1561-1593, 233-79. GI, Santo Domingo, folios 3, 4-5.

31 H. Ternaux-Compans, *Voyages, Relations et Mémoires Originaux pour Servir a L'Histoire de la Découverte de L'Amerique* (Paris, 1841), 165-232.

32 *Colección de documentos inéditos,* III, 441-79.

33 French, *Historical Collections of Louisiana and Florida,* 191-234

34 Ruidíaz, *La Florida,* II, 431-65.

My translation of the passage connected with the settlement of Florida was made from the text in Ruidíaz:

. . . we went away on the lookout for the river and port which I mentioned above, where Our Lord and His Blessed Mother were pleased that we find our flagship and another vessel. Between themselves, they [the two commanders] bad resolved to do the same thing that we did. Three companies went ashore, one being that of Captain Andrés López Patiño and the other, that of Captain Juan de San Vicente, who is a very important gentleman. They were well received by the Indians, who gave them a rather large house belonging to a chief, which is near the river shore. Immediately, Captain Patiño and Captain San Vicente, with their good industry and diligence, commanded that a moat be dug around this house, with adequate terreplein of earth and fascines, which is the material available in this land, because in all of it there is not a sign of a stone. To date, we have inside twenty-four bronze pieces, the smallest exceeding twenty-five hundredweight. Our fort is about fifteen leagues from that of the enemy. The results accomplished by the industry of these two captains were so great that, with the finger nails of their soldiers, they built a fort to defend themselves, there being no other tools. When the General came ashore, he was astonished at what they had done.

Saturday, the eighth of the said month of September, day of the Nativity of Our Lady, the General landed with many banners waving and many trumpets and other instruments of [military music], and the booming of many artillery pieces. As I had been ashore since the previous day, I took a cross and went to meet them, [singing] the hymn Te Deum Laudamus. The General and all the others who accompanied him came directly to the cross, and kneeling on the ground, kissed it. A large number of Indians were looking at all these ceremonies, and they too did everything that they saw the others do. This same day, milord the General took possession of this land for

---

35   Francisco López de Mendoza Grajales, *The Founding of St. Augustine: Memoir of the Happy Result and Prosperous Voyage of the Fleet Commanded by the Illustrious Captain-General Pedro Menendez de Aviles* (Old South Leaflets, No. 89; Boston, 1896).

His Majesty, and all the captains gave him their oath [as lord] of all this land, and as this was finished. . . [36]

Biography by Solís

The third contemporary source about the settlement of St. Augustine is the unfinished biography of Menendez by Gonzalo Solís de Merás. Solís was Menéndez's brother-in-law, came with him to Florida, and was one of the two men who actually killed Jean Ribault. Solís overlooks the latter fact, but Bartolomé Barrientos later told it. The biography describes Menéndez from his youth until his arrival back in Spain from Florida in July 1567. It was probably at this time that Solís began his writing, only to have it abruptly interrupted.[37]

From a copy of the Solís manuscript in his possession, Andrés González Barcia extracted extensively for his *Ensayo cronológico para la historia general de la Florida* (1723),[38] which was translated into English by B. F. French in 1875.[39] Ruidíaz published the complete manuscript for the first time in 1893, using the copy in possession of the Count of Revillagigedo. He supplied the text missing in this torn copy and added four chapters to complete the biography by using information from Barcia.[40] Following the text furnished by Ruidíaz, Jeannette T. Connor, in 1923, published the first full English translation of the biography by Solís. To amend gaps in the manuscript, however, Connor supplied verbatim excerpts from Barcia.[41]

My translation of the Solís account of the founding of St. Augustine is from the text in Ruidíaz:

---

[36] Ruidíaz, *La Florida,* II, 450-51.

[37] Lowery, vii; Jeannette T. Connor, *Pedro Menéndez de Avilés: Adelantado, Governor and Captain-General of Florida* (DeLand, 1923), 10-11, 12. See also the facsimile reproduction with introduction by Lyle N. McAlister (Gainesville, 1964).

[38] Lowery, *Spanish Borderlands,* ix.

[39] French, *Historical Collections of Louisiana and Florida,* 216-22.

[40] Ruidíaz, *La Florida,* I (advertencia preliminar), 1-320.

[41] Connor, *Pedro Menéndez,* 9, 245, note 2.

. . . he [Menéndez] resolved without losing time to spread sail with his flagship and to order the others to do the same. He left for the port of St. Augustine, where he arrived on the eve of Our Lady of September. Immediately after arrival, he landed up to three hundred soldiers, and sent 2 captains with them, who would immediately at daybreak next day, reconnoiter the land and the sites which seemed strongest to them, so they might speedily dig a trench [to serve] until it was decided where they could build a fort, so that when the said Adelantado landed on another day, they would show him what they had seen and resolve the most suitable thing on the matter.

And on the following day, the day of Our Lady of September, the said Adelantado landed about noon, and found many Indians who were waiting for him there, because they had heard about him from other Indians with whom he had spoken four days before. He caused a solemn mass to be said for Our Lady, and when it was finished, took possession of the land in the name of His Majesty and received solemn oath from the officials of His Majesty's royal treasury, the Fieldmaster, and the captains, that all of them would serve His Majesty with all fidelity and loyalty. This done, he caused the Indians to be fed, and the said Adelantado dined also. Immediately after finishing, he went to look at the sites which the captains he had sent had chosen for the trench, and leaving it marked out, he returned to the ships, having first held council and resolved that within 3 days everything which could be unloaded, would be taken off the ships . . . [42]

Biography by Barrientos

The biography of Menéndez written by Bartolomé Barrientos was the last recorded source. Barrientos was a professor of Latin at Salamanca University, and his penchant for mathematics earned him a reputation as a magician. He was born in Granada around 1518, but the date of his death is unknown, despite the deserved fame he enjoyed in life as a humanist. Barrientos finished his biography of Menéndez in December 1568. Since he had not been in Florida, he utilized memorials, letters, decrees, and narratives.[43]

---

[42] Ruidíaz, *La Florida,* I, 79-80.
[43] Genaro García, *Dos antiguas relaciones de la Florida* (Mexico, 1902), iii, x, xi-xii.

For many years, there was doubt about the existence of a Barrientos man-sucript since after its use as a source for a work published in 1613,[44] it had disappeared. Barcia knew it existed but was unable to locate it when he was writing his history of Florida.[45] Two historical writers in México, one in 1755 and the other in 1816, expressed doubt of its survival.[46] Then, unexpectedly in 1885, the biography was offered for sale in Madrid by the reputable book-seller, Gabriel Sanchez, and it was purchased by Don José María de Agreda Sánchez.[47]

The biography was published for the first time in 1902. Senor Agreda loaned the manuscript to Genaro García, who edited and published it for presentation at the Thirteenth International Congress of Americanists held in New York City, October 20-25, 1902.[48] The first English translation is by Anthony J. Kerrigan.[49]

This writer's translation of the passage in Barrientos concerned with the establishment of St. Augustine was made from the text furnished by García:

> That same day, the eve of Our Lady of September, the adelantado approached his port. Upon landing, he sent three hundred soldiers to reconnoiter the land and see where a trench could be dug until they resolved where they would locate a fort. The following day he disem-barked about noon, and many Indians who knew about him from others who had first seen and spoken to him were waiting. Having heard solemn mass for Our Lady, he took possession for His Majesty, swore in the officials of the Royal treasury, the field-master, and the captains, that they would serve our Catholic king in everything with the great fidelity and loyalty owed to such a lord. He saw the site cho-sen for the trench. Within three days he caused everything in the ships to be taken off . . . [50]

---

[44] Gonzalo de Illescas, *Historia pontifical y catholica* (Madrid, 1613), see García, ix-x.

[45] García, *Dos antiguas relaciones de la Florida*, x.

[46] Juan José de Eguiara y Eguren and José Mariano Berastaín y Souza respectively, see *ibid.,* iv, note 1, XI.

[47] *Ibid.,* xiv.

[48] *Ibid.,* dedicatoria, iv, 1-152.

[49] Anthony J. Kerrigan, *Pedro Menéndez* (Gainesville, publication scheduled for 1965 by the University of Florida Press).

[50] García, *Dos antiguas relaciones de la Florida*, 46.

The availability of the Spanish contemporary sources on the founding of St. Augustine and their English translations has made this event one of the best known in Florida history. This felicitous situation is manifestly the culmination of the work of several generations of students. Excerpts from the Solís biography were printed for the first time in 1723, but 152 years passed before they were translated. The publication of the complete Solís manuscript followed the excerpts 170 years later, and the complete translation, another thirty. Father López's narrative, the source next published, came out 142 years after the excerpts, but fortunately was translated within ten years. Only one year intervened between publication of the Menéndez letter in Spanish and in English. The translation, however, had been finished twenty-four years earlier. The source published last, the Barrientos biography, appeared 334 years after its writing and its translation is only just now available. Thus, the Spanish publication and English translation of the sources under consideration have been accomplished over a period of 242 years.

The rest of Spanish Florida history could be as well-known as the founding of St. Augustine were it not for the language barrier. The need, interest, and motivation are present, but inadequate linguistic knowledge often prevents direct investigation in the best Spanish sources. The rich vein of data in the University of Florida's Stetson Collection and North Carolina's Spanish Records Collection waits to be tapped. At the same time, English translations are few and far between, and the lapse between availability of source material and workable translation is excessively long. All this retards the growth of reasonably definite knowledge of an earlier phase of history, and it is Florida's pitiful loss.

Reconstruction and Analysis of the 1513 Discovery Voyage of Juan Ponce De León

Douglas T. Peck

October 1992

The long and eventful discovery voyage of Juan Ponce de León, the Spanish conquistador and explorer, has not received the amount of in-depth study and analysis that this historically significant voyage so richly deserves. Perhaps a reason for this can be found in the fact that 16th-century (and later) historians, in dwelling on the fact that the largely apocryphal purpose of the voyage was to find a fountain of youth, perverted the factual reporting of the real purpose of the voyage and its several significant discoveries. This distorted version continues in many contemporary history books because of the proclivity of writers simply to paraphrase previous authors. To avoid this I have examined original source documents wherever possible for information and data untainted by unsubstantiated conjecture and fiction.

This study documents and answers four primary questions: (1) Which island did Ponce de León visit and identify as Guanahani, the landfall of Columbus? (2) Where on the coast of Florida did Ponce de León first land? (3) Where is the Florida west coast harbor— discovered, explored, and charted by Ponce de León— that was used as a landing and departure point by later Spanish explorers? (4) Sailing southwesterly from the Tortugas, what land did Ponce de León sight and briefly explore?

The answers to these questions can be found by a reconstruction of the track of Ponce de León's voyage to determine where he made landfall on his several discoveries. This study documents such a reconstruction. A sailing vessel was used as a research test vehicle to determine the track of those segments of the voyage where the problem was one of open ocean navigation from a known departure point. The remainder of the track along the shore was determined primarily by viewing and confirming the log's description of the geographical landforms encountered.

The only extant source giving details of Ponce de León's voyage is Antonio de Herrera's *Historia General de los hechos de los Castellanos en las Islas i tierra firme del Mar Océano,* published around 1601. Philip II appointed Herrera as Spain's official historiographer of the Indies in 1592. His position gave Herrera access to both official and secret archives, and soon after Ponce de León's voyage, he must have summarized and paraphrased from the explorer's original holograph log or a copy that has since disappeared.

Used were three English translations of Herrera's chapter on Ponce de León's voyage by Florence P. Spofford, L. D. Scisco, and James E. Kelley, Jr.[1] The Kelley work includes the English translation adjacent to the Spanish text. The latter is from the original 1601 publication and contains copious footnotes explaining possible differences in interpretation of 16th-century word definitions.

Some scholars question the validity of using the navigation data in Herrera's account obtained directly from the original log. Herrera summarized and abridged Ponce de León's log in the same manner that Las Casas summarized and abridged Columbus's log. Both were done from the original holograph document or a scribe's copy. Unfortunately, Herrera added numerous comments that were based on knowledge obtained after 1513, and were missing from the original log. Thus some scholars believe that Herrera authored the entire account and that the navigational data are his and not extracted from the log. These additions by Herrera are easily identified, however, and when they are removed the original log entries of compass headings, times, distances, descriptions of landfalls, latitudes, identification of known islands with Indian names, sea conditions, and weather all of which are elements of a navigator's log come through with clarity. Why should they lose their value just because they come to us by a second person?

But what of the accuracy of the data contained in Ponce de León's log? Here there are several stumbling blocks. The latitudes for the islands and shore features do not agree with known facts. His compass courses would have put him ashore in some places, and, in others, he would have been far at sea when he reported land. There will be answers to these questions as the voyage is reconstructed, but first one must examine the purpose and goal of the voyage and determine where Juan Ponce intended to sail.

Juan Ponce de León was relieved as governor of Puerto Rico in 1511, when Don Diego Colon asserted his right to appoint governors of the Indies

---

[1] The Spofford translation is contained in T. Frederick Davis, "History of Juan Ponce de León's Voyages to Florida: Source Records," *Florida Historical Quarterly* 14 (July 1935), passim. L. D. Scisco's translation, "The Track of Ponce de León in 1513," can be found in *Bulletin of the American Geographical Society* 45 (No. 10, 1913), 721-35. Kelley's translation is from a working draft, April 15, June 7, 1990, and a final edition from July 26, 1990.

islands according to the crown's contract with Columbus. Already a very wealthy aristocrat and on good terms with the court, Juan Ponce had the insatiable urge of the Spanish conquistador to obtain more wealth and more prestige. Thus, when "he had news that they found lands to the north," he resolved to go there.[2] He applied to the king for permission to seek new lands to discover, to be named adelantado of those he conquered, and to receive the honor and wealth from his successful ventures.

The Spanish crown closely controlled permission to explore. Open-ended charters or patents were not issued, and documents spelled out specific terms, including naming the destination or goal of the planned exploration. The capitulation or patent that Ponce de León received in February 1512 detailed his authority and mission.[3] He was authorized to seek and claim the Islands of Beniny.[4] There was no mention of a fountain of youth, but the patent included detailed accounting procedures for the immense wealth that, according to Indian rumor, was present in Beniny and the surrounding islands.

The "lands to the north" and the Islands of Beniny are indicated in Peter Martyr's map of the New World published in 1511.[5] Peter Martyr, a learned historian and cosmographer in the Spanish court, undoubtedly had access to all the knowledge and reports from the Spanish discoveries, from spies, and from Portuguese, French, and English expeditions. Ponce de León probably did not have a copy of this map, but, as an aristocratic conquistador, he had access to the same sources of information used by Martyr to draw his map. The Martyr map was among the latest knowledge available at the time of Ponce de León's planned voyage, and it became a graphic picture of the "news" of which he spoke. The large land mass north of Cuba, labeled on the Martyr map as the "Isla de Beimeni parte," was the Islands of Beniny and was Ponce de León's goal according to his patent. While most of the map is greatly distorted (particularly the shore of Honduras and Nicaragua), the eastern end of Cuba, Espanola, Puerto Rico, and the Lucayos (Bahamas) are

---

2   David O. True, in "Some Early Maps Relating to Florida," *Imago Mundi* 11 (1954), 73-84, gives a comprehensive review of the lands known or suspected to exist north of Cuba prior to 1512.

3   Vicente Murga Sanz, *Juan Ponce de León* (San Juan, 1971), 100-03.

4   There are various spellings for the island: Beniny, Beimendi, Bimenei, Beimeni, and the modern term Bimini.

5   Peter Martyr's map was issued in his *Legatio Babylonica, Oceani Decas, Poemata, Epigramata* (Seville, 1511).

fairly accurately portrayed since this was the area of most intensive occupation, exploration, and charting at the time. The charts and rutters of the Lucayos Islands and adjacent waters were available to Anton de Alaminos, the professional pilot of Ponce de León's voyage. Ponce de León likely understood what he had to do to reach his goal. He would sail seaward up the chain of the Lucayos to the northernmost charted island of Guanahani and then travel across the uncharted sea in a northwesterly direction to his Islands of Beniny.

In the reconstruction of the voyage, one finds the latitudes reported by Ponce de León troublesome—particularly the latitudes of Guanahani and the landfall on the Florida coast—and they have provoked controversy concerning their accuracy. Some scholars insist that the latitudes reported in the log must be reasonably accurate because they were taken with a quadrant or astrolabe. This, however, does not square with the knowledge that we have of early 16th-century Spanish navigation.

Ponce de León was neither a seaman nor a navigator. He was an aristocratic conquistador, trained from early childhood as a warrior, and he spent most of his adult life fighting the Moors in Africa, the rebellious Tainos on Espanola, and the Caribs on Puerto Rico and adjacent islands. The king's patent required him to keep a log to establish his claim to the islands he discovered. He no doubt wrote the narrative portion of that log, but he likely turned to Alaminos for the navigational data of latitudes and compass courses. Anton de Alaminos was an "up from the ranks" Spanish pilot who had served as a young apprentice seaman with Columbus on one of his early voyages and had stayed in the Caribbean to become the most experienced and sought-after pilot in the Indies. And like all Spanish pilots of his time, his simple, unlettered trade consisted of navigation by dead reckoning (compass course and distance) from a known departure point. Yet some scholars picture him as proficient in celestial navigation and taking sights on the meridian of the sun. Edward Lawson argues that Alaminos must have used an obsolete edition of the tables of declination, but there is no indication in the log that either Alaminos or Juan Ponce used celestial navigation. This required expertise in the use of an astrolabe and the complicated tables of declination in a current Regiomontanus Ephemerides or Kalendarius, both of which were written in Latin.[6]

---

[6] Edward W. Lawson, *The First Landing Place of Juan Ponce de León on the North American Continent in the Year 1513* (St. Augustine, 1956).

After intensive research into the subject, Samuel Eliot Morison notes: "Celestial navigation formed no part of the professional pilot's or master's training in Columbus' day or for long after his death. It was practiced only by men of learning such as mathematicians, astrologers, physicians, or by gentlemen of education."[7] Alaminos was none of these, so it can be concluded that he used only dead reckoning to determine his azimuth position and latitude. Alaminos's use of dead reckoning to establish his latitudes will be further developed in the reconstruction to follow.

The compass courses given in the log are also troublesome, and for this one needs to examine the magnetic variation of the area in question and the variation correction, if any, set into the compass being used.[8] In developing both plotted and sailed courses, I used the magnetic variation for the early 16th century, projected by James E. Kelley, Jr., from a computer analysis of early charts, maps, rutters, and other documents.[9] Compasses of the time were made in various European cities, and it was common practice for the compass to be set to true north when manufactured, thus building into the compass the variation correction for that particular city. Kelley also deduces from a study of early maritime navigation that the Spanish explorers of the period used a compass made in Seville with a one-half point (5.63 degrees) easterly correction built in. This correction (I should say error), built in by the manufacturer, shifted the north arrow on the card point to the left, or counterclockwise, 5.6 degrees from magnetic north. On a voyage, then, when magnetic north is moved farther to the left (as in a westerly variation zone), the north arrow on the card will be rotated to the left from true north to the degree of the westerly variation. Accordingly, I applied this 5.6 degree correction of the Seville compass to my navigational computations.

After outfitting three vessels at his own expense, as spelled out in the patent, Ponce de León departed from Anasco Bay the afternoon of March 3, 1513, in search of the Islands of Beniny. His pilot, Alaminos, without a doubt had with him a chart of the Lucayos Islands, at least as far north as Guanahani. Beyond that point lay unexplored islands. Passing Point Borinquen (then called Point Aguada), Ponce de León took his departure for naviga-

7   Samuel Eliot Morison, *Admiral of the Ocean Sea: A Life of Christopher Columbus* (Boston, 1942), 183-96.

8   Magnetic variation is the difference in degrees between magnetic north and true (geographical) north.

9   James E. Kelley, Jr., letter to author, April 22, 1990.

tional purposes sometime after midnight, March 5. He reported sailing a heading of northwest by north to his first landfall in the Turks and Caicos islands. It is this northwest-by-north heading that must now be corrected so the track can be accurately sailed to identify the reported island landfalls.

The compass heading of northwest by north on the thirty-two-point compass then in use comes out to 326.25 degrees. When computed for the built-in Seville variation correction, it is 326.25 - 5.63 = 320.62 degrees. By rounding off the decimals to 321 degrees, one has the compass (or magnetic) heading that Juan Ponce sailed.[10]

But the compass heading that Ponce de León traveled was not the actual, true heading that I needed to compute for the compass heading I should sail for my reconstruction. This basic 321 degree compass heading had to be further corrected for the westerly variation on each leg, and since the first leg had a westerly variation of five degrees, the computation is 321 - 5 = 316 degrees. This 316 degrees is the true heading (from true north) of the first leg to be sailed to arrive at the true course or track over the bottom as influenced by the currents. This computation was repeated for each leg as the basic compass headings and/or variation changes.

I sailed the first leg for three and one-half days, or eighty-four hours, to an island on the Banks of the Babueca, named El Viejo, which can be positively identified as Grand Turk Island.

It is the only island on a large bank near the end of both the sailed and reconstructed track. The distance to Grand Turk is 288 nautical miles. The time of eighty-four hours computes to a speed of 3.4 knots over the bottom. With the help of the Antilles current (around 0.8 knots), this computes to a speed of 2.6 knots through the water—a reasonable speed for Ponce de León's heavy—laden vessels.

The chart in Figure 1 shows the plotted track from Puerto Rico with each individual plot between the islands that Ponce de León either sighted or at which he anchored. The track shown is that sailed on the corrected true heading as influenced by the Antilles current.

My sailed track was bent considerably to the west of the 316 degree heading by the branch of the Antilles current that flows westerly past Hispaniola and Cuba, and I ended three nautical miles northeast of Grand Turk Island. I believe that Ponce de León reached the bank five to seven miles east of my

---

[10]   Unlike our present compass rose, or card, which is divided into 360 degrees, the early 16th-century compass rose was divided into 32 points, or segments, equaling 11.25 degrees.

position, since he reported anchoring on the bank (Banks of Babueca) that stretches almost twenty miles in a southwesterly direction from Grand Turk. On such a long leg, and considering all the variables, my track verifies not only Ponce de León's reported compass heading and distance but also verifies the correction factors that I used to correct the heading for 16th-century conditions.

Juan Ponce's log gives the latitude of El Viejo as 22 degrees, 30 minutes N., while the actual latitude of Grand Turk is 21 degrees, 25 minutes N. (from the anchorage on the bank, south). Placement of the latitude a little over one degree too far north will be reflected slightly differently in all later latitude reports in the log. This is because Alaminos started his dead reckoning from Point Aguada with a northerly error on his chart, and early 16th-century charts and rutters consistently show known landmarks in the New World as several degrees too far north. The Rotz chart, as late as 1542, shows the Puerto Rico latitude nearly three degrees too far north.[11]

After the sail to El Viejo, Juan Ponce passed the next several islands to reach his immediate destination of Guanahani, from which he then moved into unknown waters in search of the Islands of Beniny. Precise navigation is not required here, and the islands are identified primarily by their being a day's sailing distance in a northwesterly direction.

Juan Ponce's log then reads: "The next day they anchored at an islet of the Lucayos, called Caycos." This is East Caicos, one of the few islands that retained its Indian name. The following day's entry notes: "Soon they anchored at another called Yaguna in 24 degrees." This is identified as North Caicos—an easy day's sail of about thirty-five miles, as indicated by the expression "soon they anchored." The north shore of North Caicos is at latitude 21 degrees, 58 minutes N., indicating that Alaminos carried forward the northerly error from his departure point, with the error gradually increasing. This increase in error can be explained in part by the fact that Alaminos was unaware of the increasing westerly variation bending his compass heading to the south. He likely thought he was traveling on a more northerly course.

The log continues: "At the 11th of the same [month] they came to another island called Amaguayo, and there they stayed al reparo." As the chart shows, sailing the corrected compass heading for about forty-eight nautical miles—an overnight sail at 2.6 knots—brought Juan Ponce to Mayaguana.

---

11   Jean Rotz, *The Boke of Idrography* (London, 1542; reprint edited by Helen Wallis, New York, 1981).

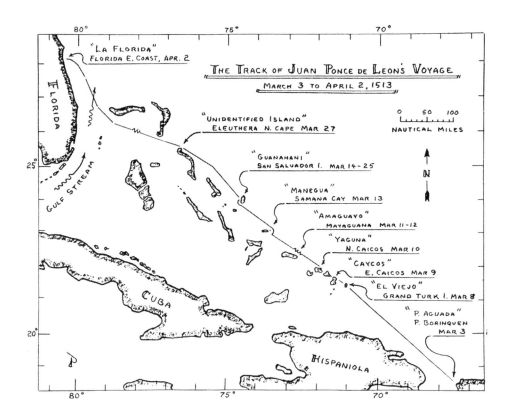

Most scholars in previous translations conclude that they anchored here for "repairs," but Kelley correctly shows that "al reparo" means hove-to, or as in Columbus's diario, "jogging on and off."

From here Ponce de León sailed to an island called "Manegua," which he apparently passed without stopping, locating it at 24 degrees, 30 minutes N. latitude. As the chart shows, this is Samana Cay, whose latitude is 23 degrees, 03 minutes N. Once again the location shows that Alaminos, by the dead reckoning, retained the northerly error. Samana is the small cay that the National Geographic Society named Guanahani—the landfall of Columbus—but the Ponce de León log has him arriving at Guanahani the next day and about sixty-five nautical miles farther on the northwesterly course. The Jean Rotz chart also shows Manegua (Samana Cay) as being southeast of Guanahani.

The next leg carried Ponce de León to the island of San Salvador, and the log entry contains several significant facts: "At the 14th they came to Guanahani, which lies in 25 degrees, 40 minutes, where they trimmed up one ship in order to cross the windward sea of those islands of the Lucayos." Ponce de León identified the island as the one that "Admiral Don Christoval Colon discovered."

At a later date the log calls out the latitude of Key West as 1 degree, 40 minutes too far north, which is about the average of the northerly errors from dead reckoning. If this 1 degree, 40 minute northerly error is subtracted from the 25 degrees, 40 minutes reported for Guanahani, the result is 24 degrees latitude, which locates it through the middle of San Salvador. This revelation enters Ponce de León into the current controversy over the landfall of Columbus by identifying it as the island of San Salvador.

Another fact at this point is that Ponce de León changed his course to the northwest, prepared the ships for an ocean crossing (the "windward sea") from the Lucayos, and was ready to move into unknown seas in search of his Islands of Beniny. This scenario can be seen in the Peter Martyr map (Figure 2), where the landmass titled "Isla de Beimeni" lies in a northwest direction over open water from the northernmost charted island (Guanahani) of the Lucayos.

At this point my reconstruction returns to using my sailing vessel to duplicate the track over open water from Guanahani to Ponce de León's landfall on the shore of Florida. The party departed Guanahani probably on March 25 and ran northwest until March 27. At this point Juan Ponce and his pilot saw an island that they could not identify—no doubt because it was not on their chart. The northwest heading of 315 degrees when corrected for the 5.6 degree Seville compass factor and the 9 degree westerly variation becomes 300 degrees true.

My track, pushed north by the strong Antilles current in this area, ran about fifteen nautical miles east of Cat Island and into the northwest trending coast of northern Eleuthera. This track shows that Eleuthera was the island "they could not identify," and they probably rounded it to the north at Bridge Point and resumed their northwest heading.

Nearly all previous research has Ponce de León sailing around Great Abaco, indicating it as the island the Spaniards saw but could not identify. This is a natural conclusion because of the long chain of Bahamas Islands lying in a generally northwesterly direction, and Great Abaco is the last island before open waters across to the east coast of Florida. I had assumed my track would follow this same route, so when my sailed track from San Salvador ran into Eleuthera, far from the cape I had assumed I would round

PETER MARTYR'S MAP OF THE NEW WORLD

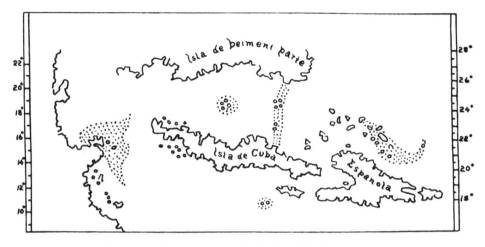

This is a scaled reproduction of the northeast portion
of Peter Martyr's map issued in his "Legatio Babylonica,
Oceani Decas, Poemata, Epigrammata, at Seville in 1511.

Projected latitudes not present on original map are added, and
the label "Isla de Beimeni" printed right side up for clarity

before sailing to Florida, I thought my project was in trouble because of bad course correction factors.

But my calculations had worked for over 700 miles and had pinpointed six of the islands scattered through the Bahamas. Why would they fail now? I soon realized that Great Abaco was not the turning point toward Florida; it had to be Bridge Point on Eleuthera.

On Monday, March 28, Ponce de León left Bridge Point on Eleuthera astern and continued sailing on a northwest heading. His log reads: "They ran 15 leagues by the same course, and Wednesday they proceeded in the same way."[12] This means that for two twenty-four-hour sailing days they ran northwest fifteen leagues (about forty-five miles) each day. The speed computes to less than two knots (1.87) per day.

I believe this reduced speed was deliberate. Alaminos and Ponce de León were sailing into unknown, uncharted waters. They had already been surprised to see an unknown and uncharted island. This was not the time to rush headlong and perhaps end up on a reef. I believe they intentionally

---

[12]   Interpretations of the length of one Spanish league vary from 2.82 to 3.40 nautical miles. For my computations, I used an arbitrary factor of 3.0 nautical miles for each league.

slowed their progress, constantly sounded with the lead, and probably hoved-to at night or in times of restricted visibility, especially in view of the fact that they were sailing into a period of dark nights with a waning moon.[13] This track from Eleuthera to the coast of Florida is shown in Figure 3.

To maintain the reduced speed, I sailed the corrected heading of 297 degrees true with drastically reduced sails for ninety miles, and I found that on this heading the strong Antilles current, which turns and flows through New Providence channel, carried me right through this wide channel about ten miles south of the southern cape of Great Abaco. Since Juan Ponce had seen Eleuthera in daylight, he would have passed Great Abaco after dark, although he could not have seen it at ten miles distance even in daylight.

My reconstructed track passed within the theoretical sighting range of both Cat Island and Great Abaco, but I did not see either landmass, and neither did Ponce de León. The theoretical sighting range is based upon a viewer's line of sight passing just inches over the curvature of the earth's horizon and picking up the top few inches of the highest elevation on an island in unlimited visibility. Far more than the top few inches of an island must be above the horizon for the naked eye to see it, and unlimited visibility never exists in the Bahamas, especially in the summer months when a heavy sea haze is present. For this reason, even though my chart appeared to have Ponce de León sailing through a maze of several islands, he was unable to see them and thought he was in the open sea headed for Beniny.

At this point (March 29) the log reads: "And afterwards, with bad weather, up to 2 April, running west-northwest, the water [depth] decreased to 9 brazas, at one league from shore."

Here Juan Ponce and his party obviously ran into a cold front, with the accompanying storms and wind shift to the northerly quadrant, forcing them to change course to west-northwest. During the initial passage of the front on March 29-March 30, when the wind came out strong from the northwest and north, he likely did what any prudent sailor would do. He hoved-to, or jogged along, barely moving under reduced sail. After about twenty-four hours, when the winds shifted to the northeast and the storms abated, Ponce de León was able to pick up that west-northwest heading. With this heading he probably was hard on the wind rather than running with the wind as before, and since a square-rigged vessel of that era simply did not respond well to windward work, his forward progress was likely

---

[13]   Herman H. Goldstine, *New and Full Moons 1001 B.C. to A.D. 1651* (Philadelphia, 1973).

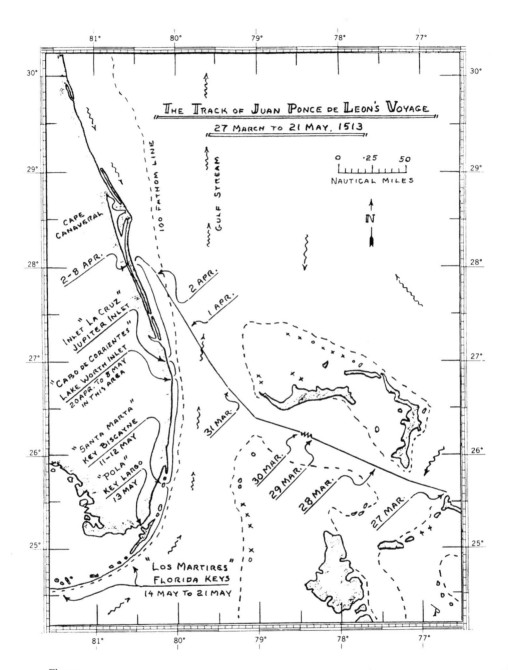

Figure 3

reduced to a crawl. This, combined with cautious jogging at night, likely reduced Ponce de León's forward progress to about thirty miles a day or less.

The Spanish probably crossed the Gulf Stream at its strongest point where it is squeezed between the lower bulge of Florida and the protruding Great Bahamas Bank, and, in this venturi, the current can and does pick up speeds of over three knots. During my sailing of this track I experienced a 3.8 knot current for over twelve hours between Grand Bahamas and Florida, with the current averaging 1.5-2.5 knots on either side of that point. With the slow progress of the vessels, they probably were swept north faster than their progress west, and this is reflected in the track.

On April 1 Ponce de León and his crew were in the strongest part of the Gulf Stream, being swept north. Then early on April 2, as they reached the 100 fathom line and moved out of the strongest current, the course began to veer more westerly, and they reached their landfall and subsequent anchorage later that day.

From my reconstructed track I found that Ponce de León's anchorage and landing after discovering Florida and the North American continent were about 28 degrees N. latitude and 80 degrees, 29 minutes W. longitude, which is below Cape Canaveral and a short distance south of Melbourne Beach. I do not say that this is the exact spot, but I place the accuracy within five to eight nautical miles either side of this fix.

After landfall Ponce de León ran along the coast looking for an inlet or harbor, and, not finding one, he anchored in eight brazas of water.[14] The log is ambiguous as to whether he ran along the coast in a northly or southly direction, but the question is moot since he could not have gone far before nightfall forced him to anchor. At my projected site, based on the log, the description of the coastline fits, and the depth of water for the anchorage is within a few feet of that reported.

Alaminos placed this point at 30 degrees, 08 minutes latitude or 2 degrees, 05 minutes north of my position. This northerly error is consistent with Alaminos's gradually increasing northerly errors in reporting the latitudes of the islands to this point in the northwesterly track.

---

[14]   Spofford and Scisco both translate *braza* as fathom (six feet). Kelley identifies a Spanish braza as equivalent to 5.5 English feet. This means that Juan Ponce anchored in about forty-four feet of water. Researchers who use the standard six-foot fathom calculate the depth at fifty-four feet.

If one accepts the logical, reasonable, rational, and indeed proven point that Alaminos's dead reckoning, as influenced by the unknown currents and magnetic variation, was not an exact science, then it can be shown that Alaminos's latitudes, with their ever-increasing northerly errors, explain why once again he reported his latitude a considerable distance north of his actual landfall. Advocates of a St. Augustine landing site, with strained and incongruous reasoning, insist that of the ten latitudes given by Alaminos, containing northerly errors, it was the only one with an accurate celestial navigation position without the northerly error.

After finding nothing of interest ashore, or perhaps waiting for a favorable wind, Ponce de León left the anchorage on April 8 and sailed slowly south along the coast, no doubt anchoring each night. For twelve days he reported no inlets, capes, or Indian villages, which is consistent with the smooth and relatively barren coast south of the landfall at twenty-eight degrees latitude. On April 21 he ran into the strong Gulf Stream current near shore. At this location, which I have identified as a point just north of Lake Worth Inlet, the stream pushed him back faster than he could sail forward, although he reported that he had good winds. Ponce de León managed to anchor his ship and one other, but the third ship was caught offshore in water too deep to anchor and was carried back north out of sight.

This action could only have taken place at the bulge (or cape) of the coast just north of Lake Worth Inlet. I experienced a 2.3 knot current when sailing past this point, and it could be greater if influenced by tidal flow, surface air temperature, and pressure gradients. At this point, the twenty-fathom line (too deep for anchoring) comes within one and one-half miles of shore, and the shallow shelf for anchoring falls off rapidly rather than gradually, as it does farther north. The third ship could have been within a few hundred feet of the two that anchored, but, unable to anchor, it was carried north by the current.

This scenario cannot be repeated north of Cape Canaveral as the bottom there gets deeper only gradually, providing ample anchoring depths as far as twenty miles offshore. This rules out a landfall above that point since Ponce de León likely stayed inshore in sight of land. In following the coast south, the first cape he would have reached was Cape Canaveral, and these conditions do not exist there.

At this point Juan Ponce landed ashore and, after a fight with the Indians, "departed from there to a river, where he took on water and firewood." The river was Jupiter Inlet, which he no doubt had seen when he passed it earlier. He named this river "La Cruz" and left a stone cross with an inscription. He must have stayed here for some time waiting for the return of the third ship and for enough wind to fight the strong current, as the next entry is May 8. It reads: "Sunday, 8 May they doubled the cape of La Florida, which they called Cabo de Corrientes."

This is the cape below Jupiter Inlet where the Spaniards had previously experienced the strong currents carrying away the third ship, so naturally they called it "Cabo de Corrientes." Herrera muddied the water here by inserting his own interpretation that they were doubling the "cape of La Florida," which was on maps of his time (usually at Biscayne Bay), but in fact they were still north of this point.

The log entry continues: "All this coast, from Punta de Arracifes, to Cabo de Corrientes, runs north by northwest and south by southeast and is clean, and of depth of 6 brazas and the cape lies in 28 degrees, 15 minutes." The coast to "Cabo de Corrientes" does run north by northwest and south by southeast and is clean, but where is "Punta de Arracifes?" Ponce de León had not mentioned this landmark before. This is another insertion by Herrera from a later map and should be disregarded; he may have it incorrectly located, as he did cape La Florida.

Alaminos reports this cape at latitude 28 degrees, 15 minutes while it is actually at 26 degrees, 48 minutes. Alaminos was now shortening his northerly error to 1 degree, 27 minutes, and that is understandable since his calculations were based upon his estimate of speed and distance from fifteen different, short, slow-moving legs in unknown currents.

From this point, "they navigated until they found two islands to the south in 27 degrees, to one which had a league of unimpaired shoreline, they assigned the name Santa Marta, they took on water at her." Santa Marta is Key Biscayne, which has a little over a league (three and one-half miles) of unimpaired shoreline, and the other island is Virginia Key. These are the first two islands south of Lake Worth Inlet (Cabo de Corrientes).

Alaminos reports the latitude of Santa Marta at 27 degrees when it actually lies at 25 degrees, 42 minutes, which indicates that he was now calculating his latitude 1 degree, 18 minutes too far north. The errors in his last two calculated latitudes were probably due to his inability to estimate these strong and changing currents since the variation would not have been as great a factor on this southerly course as it was on the northwesterly course.

The next entry reads: "Friday 13 May, they made sail, running along the edge of a sandbank, and reef of islands, as far as an island they call Pola, which lies in 26 degrees, 30 minutes and between the shoal and the reef of islands, and the mainland it extends toward the great sea like a bay." Pola is probably Key Largo. Ponce de León was running down Hawk Channel between the outer reef and the Keys, and through the several inlets he could see the eastern extremity of Florida Bay, which Herrera knew extended into the "Great Sea," or Gulf of Mexico. The latitude here is meaningless since Key Largo is such a long island, extending north-northeast and south-south-west, and the latitude could vary by over one-half a degree depending upon where it was measured.

Starting here, the log is vague as to specific islands, but it is apparent that Ponce de León continued down Hawk Channel to the Tortugas, naming the string of keys "Los Martires." Alaminos reported the keys at latitude 26 degrees, 15 minutes, and Key West and the adjacent keys at 24 degrees, 35 minutes. His northerly error now became 1 degree, 40 minutes—about the midpoint of the range of his northerly errors.

The log at this point is unclear and is obviously missing some lines, but it implies that on May 21 the party turned "sometimes to the north and at others to the northeast," and, although the departure point is not mentioned, this turn was made at the Tortugas. This is when Ponce de León turned north and east to explore the backside of his island, and since one cannot pinpoint his place of landing by a reconstruction of the track from such vague compass headings, one must rely on the geographical description of that landfall.

On May 23 the log reads: "They ran along the coast, to the south (not caring to see what was Mainland) as far as some islets, which were running out to sea, and because it seemed there was an entrance, between them, and the coast, for the ships, in order to take on water and firewood, they stayed there until 3 June, and careened one ship." The obvious landfall here is on the mainland just north of Gasparilla Island where Ponce de León sailed south past the islands of La Costa, Captiva, and Sanibel to the wide and deep entrance to San Carlos Bay at the mouth of the Caloosahatchee River. This landfall fits the north and northeasterly sailing directions and the geographical description of the islands.

The Spaniards found the harbor (San Carlos Bay), which they later reconnoitered. There was ample anchorage with nearby protected shelving beaches upon which the boats could be careened. Charlotte Harbor has been proposed as the harbor they explored, but that location is a large, shallow, almost landlocked inland bay with only a tortuous, winding, dredged entrance through nearly three miles of offshore shoals. It hardly justifies the name harbor.

Ponce de León remained in the harbor for nine days. There were skirmishes with well-organized Indians who put up fierce resistance. He captured four of the natives, released two, and kept the others as guides. The Spanish departed on June 14, stopping by a nearby island (probably Sanibel) for firewood and water.

Ponce de León seemingly had gained little, but Alaminos, in one of his responsibilities as pilot, charted the harbor. It became a key issue in later exploration of the mainland. During the reconnoiter of the harbor on June 5, Alaminos likely noted that the wide, deep mouth of the Caloosahatchee River, where it empties into San Carlos Bay, could accommodate many deep-draft vessels. He also found on the south side of the river, at what is now Punta Rassa, a deep spot right at the shore where the vessels could tie up as at a wharf and unload heavy equipment and horses.

While Spanish pilots were ordered to keep their charts secret from the French and the English, after 1513 the Alaminos chart was common knowledge to other Spanish pilots operating in the area. This deep-water port was utilized by Alonzo Alvarez de Pineda in 1518, by the re-supply ship of Panfilo Narváez in 1527, and is the most logical known deep-water port for the large expeditionary force of Hernando de Soto in 1539.

Leaving San Carlos Bay, Ponce de León reached the Tortugas on June 21, where he provisioned his ships with fresh meat and took aboard 160 loggerhead turtles that were nesting there. Three days later, on June 24, he decided to sail on a course southwest by west.

At this point one must question why he had abandoned his search to the north and selected the southwest-by-west route. All his other courses across unknown waters in search of Beniny had been to the north, so why now sail such a finite course and in a direction contrary to his belief that Beniny lay somewhere north of the Lucayos?

One can only conclude that the Indians convinced him that the rich lands that he sought were not to the north. They pointed southwest by west, straight to the Yucatan. The two Indian guides he captured in San Carlos Bay may have been a factor in this change of course.

This leg of the voyage is critical in determining exactly where Ponce de León landed after sailing this new course for two and one-half days. Also this is one of the legs where use of a sailing vessel to arrive at the true track over the bottom is superior to attempting to plot the track using non-empirical estimates for the influence of the currents.

The following is the computation of my compass heading: on the thirty-two-point compass, southwest by west is 236.25 degrees. After subtracting the Seville compass error, it becomes 236.25 - 5.63 = 230.62 degrees. Adding the two degree easterly variation, it becomes 230.62 + 2 = 232.62, or 233 degrees for the true heading sailed. I sailed on this heading at a speed of 2.6 knots. By computing the time and distance of previous legs, I determined that this was Ponce de León's average speed with favorable wind conditions. He may have sailed slower and more cautiously at night and faster during the day, but use of this average speed, while affecting the enroute track slightly, would have put him in the same location.

My recorded track over the bottom is illustrated in Figure 4. I recorded a Sat Nav and a Loran C fix every four hours.[15] The fixes are numbered for convenience of analysis. One will notice that the loop current from the northwest began almost immediately, pushing my vessel south of the sailed heading. In fixes seven through eleven I reached the axis of the Gulf Stream, the track actually was pushed back east, and the four hour distance over the bottom was cut nearly in half. Beginning at fix eleven and through fix thirteen, the current diminished, the course picked up a more westerly vector, and the distance over the bottom increased. I terminated my sailed track twelve miles from the coast of Cuba as required by State Department regulation.

I determined that Ponce de León's track probably ended fifty-eight nautical miles west of Havana, just west of a harbor at Bahia Hondu and on the ten-fathom shelf where there would have been ample anchorage sites for his brief exploration of the coast. At this spot Ponce de León could not decide whether this was Cuba or some new, unknown land. While the Spanish occupied the extreme eastern end of Cuba, the central and western area was an unknown and unexplored wilderness, and Ponce de León likely could not identify it. The Spanish do mention Cuba, but only with a confusing and ambiguous statement: "They found themselves 18 full leagues abaft the beam for it to be Cuba."[16] Does this mean it was not Cuba because it was

---

15   Sat Nav (Satellite Navigation System) supplies an accurate latitude/longitude fix upon passage of any one of twelve orbiting satellites. Loran C (Long Range Navigation System) is based on shore-transmitted signals. It gives a continuous, accurate latitude/longitude fix and computerized log and speed over the bottom.

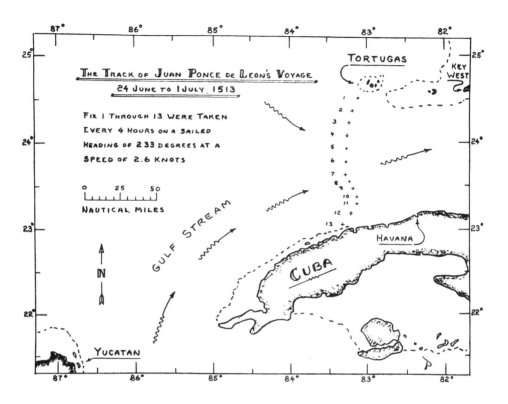

located eighteen leagues (about fifty-four nautical miles) in the wrong direction? This seems a small error in view of their extensive voyage from any known landmark. We will probably never know what was meant by this remark, and esoteric conjecture about it serves no useful purpose.

Some historians contend that Ponce de León did reach the Yucatan on this leg and so became the discoverer of Mexico.[17] They overlook the fact, however, that Ponce de León would have had to sail at a speed of 6.76 knots to

---

16 This is Kelley's translation. Spofford translates the phrase as "off course," which is equally ambiguous.

17 The most prominent of these works is Samuel Eliot Morison's *European Discovery of America: The Southern Voyages, A.D. 1492-1616* (New York, 1974), 499-536. See also Aurelio Tió, "Historia del descubrimiento de la Florida y Beimeni o Yucatan," *Historia Boletín* 2 (no. 8, 1972). Both authors base their opinions on depositions in court records many years after the fact in which petitioners (probably Ponce de León's surviving relatives) tried to establish land grants in the Yucatan. This is hardly a valid source for establishing a historical event involving landfall of a sailing vessel for which the navigation log exists.

make the 300 miles against an average current of 1.5 knots. This speed was not only quite unattainable for their vessels, but rather than the southwest-by-west heading reported, he would have been forced to sail a heading of 260 degrees for the first half of the leg—to avoid being swept down to Cuba—then, about midway, change to a heading of 205 degrees to make the Yucatan. This is a highly unlikely scenario.

Ponce de León, after briefly exploring the coast of Cuba, no doubt deciding it was not Beniny, and probably running short of both provisions and patience, left Cuba on July 1 for the return to Puerto Rico. He elected to retrace his route through the northern Lucayos because of his obsession that Beniny was located there. As a last desperate effort before returning to Puerto Rico, he sent one ship with Juan Perez de Ortubio as captain and Anton de Alaminos as pilot to search again the northern Lucayos for Beniny.

Ponce de León reached Puerto Rico around the middle of October without finding his island. Ortubio and Alaminos returned a short time later and, after discovering a large wooded island (probably Andros), announced that it was Beniny. Everyone concerned must have realized that it was just another of the primitive, windswept Lucayos islands inhabited by a few poor and frightened Taino Indians. Nevertheless, this pronouncement resulted in cartographers introducing the island's name into the northeastern section of the Bahamas where it was changed often. Eventually, they designated it as the present island of Bimini east of Miami.

Juan Ponce de León failed to find his Islands of Beniny. He died in 1521 at the age of forty-seven without realizing that he had contributed much to future Spanish exploration and conquest of the mainland. He had discovered the Gulf Stream—vital in carrying the treasure-laden Spanish galLeóns back to Spain—and he had also discovered the first good, deep-water harbor on the mainland, which would be used to advantage by later explorers. Finally, he gave the name La Florida to the Florida peninsula, and this became the basis for the claim of Spanish sovereignty over most of North America.

Revisiting the Freducci Map:
A Description of Juan Ponce De León's
1513 Florida Voyage?

Jerald T. Milanich and Nara B. Milanich

Winter 1996

For more than a century scholars have been aware of the Conte Ottomanno Freducci map believed to have been drafted in 1514-1515. Centered on the Atlantic Ocean with the west coasts of Europe and Africa shown, the map shows those parts of the Americas known to Europe by c. 1514-1515, including coastal Newfoundland, the Bahamas and the Caribbean Islands, and the Caribbean and Atlantic coasts of South America from present-day Gulf of Venezuela east and southeast to northeastern Brazil (the latter not very accurately). The map also seemingly accurately renders portions of the Atlantic and lower Gulf coasts of Florida. Both the portion of Florida shown and the place names affixed there appear to correlate with the 1513 voyage of Juan Ponce de León as reported in Herrera's account of that expedition first published in 1601.[1]

Geographer David O. True wrote about the Freducci map in 1944, also mentioning it in a second article he published in 1955 in which he characterized it as "probably one of the ten most important maps of Florida."[2] In both of these articles True pointed out the relevance of the map for tracing Juan Ponce de León's initial voyage to Florida. Yet in the ensuing half century since True first wrote about it, the Freducci map has escaped the attention of

---

[1] Antonio de Herrera y Tordesillas, *Historia General de los Hechos & los Castellanos, en las Islas y Tierra-Firme el Mar Océano* Vol. 2 (Buenos Aires, 1944), 207-2121; also see Frederick T. Davis, "Juan Ponce de León's Voyage to Florida," *Florida Historical Quarterly* 14 (1935), 5-70.

[2] David O. True, "The Freducci Map of 1514-1515, What it Discloses of Early Florida History," *Tequesta* 4 (November 1944), 50-55; idem, "Some Early Maps Relating to Florida," *Imago Mundi* XI (1955), 79-80. In the earlier article (p. 50) True notes that the map was reproduced in Italian, German, and French sources as early as 1892. It also was the subject of an article by Louis D. Scisco, "The Track of Ponce de Léon in 1513," *Bulletin of the American Geographical Society* XLV (1913), 721-735. We have not seen the Scisco article.

scholars tracing that voyage. Our intent in writing this article is to make the existence of the map known to scholars working in the early colonial period in Florida and to offer additional possible interpretations of the Florida portion of the map.

The entire Freducci map recently was reproduced in color in an elephant folio-sized volume entitled (in English) "Columbian Atlas of the Great Discovery," published in 1992 by the Italian Ministry of Cultural and Environmental Affairs' National Committee for the Celebration of the Quincentenary of the Discovery of America. The atlas, assembled and annotated by Osvaldo Baldacci, reproduces and provides background information on a number of maps that show the Americas and which are curated in Italian archives and libraries.[3]

The text accompanying the map notes it was drawn by the Count of Ottomanno Freducci, a cartographer active from 1497-1539. Freducci was one of a family of mapmakers who were producing maps in the 15th and 16th centuries in Ancona.

Made of two pieces of parchment glued together and measuring 1.04 by 1.20 meters, the Freducci map is in the Portolan style. Such maps were typically sea charts known for accurate portrayal of coastal configurations but notorious for inaccurate latitudes.[4] As on most Portolan maps, the Freducci map features loxodromes or rhumb lines, straight lines that indicate wind directions. These lines often intersect in elaborate compass roses.

In 1891 the Freducci map was transferred from the Pio Institute of Bardi to the State Archives in Florence, Italy. Archives in the Pio Institute are associated with one of Florence's famous noble families who, Baldacci speculates, may have commissioned the map because of the family's interest in the geography of trade markets that were beginning to open in the Americas.

Baldacci dates the map to 1514-1515, reasoning that its depiction of Florida derives from information gathered during Juan Ponce's explorations in March to September of 1513, information rapidly remitted to Europe. Moreover, he argues, it could not have been drawn much later than 1514 or 1515, since it does not depict the Pacific Ocean, which was reached by Vasco de Balboa in September 1513.

---

3   Osvaldo Baldacci, *Atlante Colombiano della Grande Scoperta* (Rome, 1992), 123-126.
4   See R.V. Tooley, *Maps and Map Makers*, 7th edition (New York, 1987), 15.

REVISITING THE FREDUCCI MAP

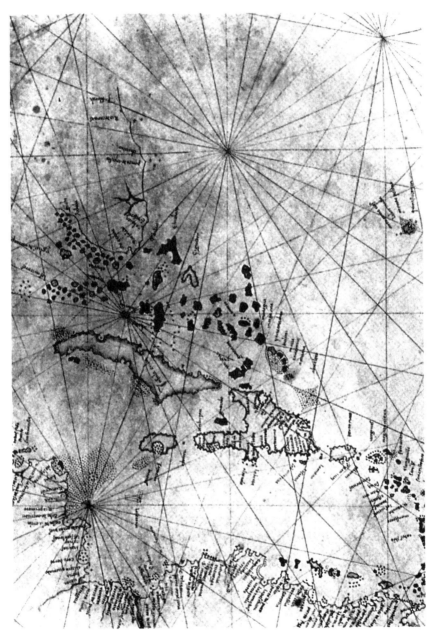

A portion of the Freducci map showing the northern coast of South America; Cuba, Hispaniola and other Caribbean islands; the Bahamas; and, at the top, Florida.

105

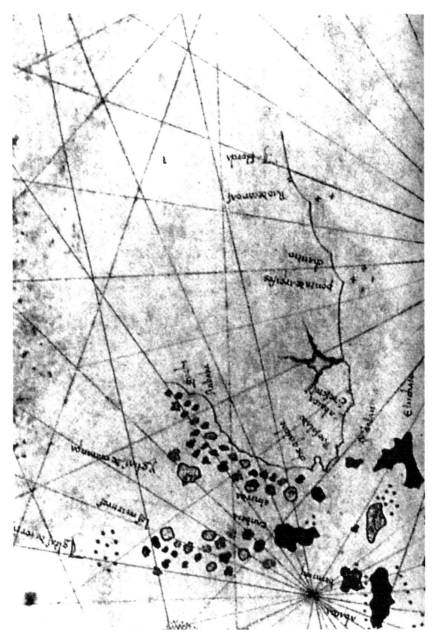

Enlargement of the Florida portion of the Freducci map. The Atlantic coast place names (upside down) from top to bottom are: *i. florda, Rio de canoas, chantio, ponta de arçifes, c. de setos, abacoa, Rio salada,* and *chequiche.* On the Gulf coast are *stababa* and *guchi* (or *juchi*).

Unfortunately the section of the map with its date of creation has been cut off. However, the other portions of the Americas shown on the map are consistent with the 1514-1515 date. Portions of the map are said by Baldacci to be based on older maps from the Ancona school. Some of those features are inaccurate, such as the depiction of an imaginary, crescent-shaped island called *bracil,* located in the North Atlantic off Ireland.

On the Freducci map the northernmost place name on the Atlantic coast of Florida is *I. [Insula] flor[i]da,* or "Island of Florida," the name which Juan Ponce de León gave to the land.[5] The location of that name presumably marks Juan Ponce's initial landfall and is consistent with his belief that Florida was an island. True notes that the position of that place name falls between Matanzas Inlet and Mosquito Inlet, suggesting the landfall was in that same general section of the coast.[6] This is consistent with most interpretations of the Herrera account of Juan Ponce's voyage.[7]

Moving southward, the next place name is *Rio de canoas,* "River of Canoes," which apparently is the name given to a river emptying into the Atlantic north of Cape Canaveral. Both True and Scisco suggest this marks the Indian River. Further south is an unlabeled cape, possibly Cape Canaveral, which the 1601 Herrera account calls *Cabo de Corrientes.*[8]

Further south on the Freducci map are two more capes. The northern one, labeled *chantio,* is certainly the *cautio* of Herrera, who claims it was the name the Lucayan Indians, the native inhabitants of the Bahamas, gave to Florida.[9] The second cape is *ponta de arcifes,* "Point of Reefs," which Herrera calls the *Punta de Arracifes.* We suggest that these two capes, both noticeable to the members of the expedition as they sailed southward, could have been Sewalls Point just north of St. Lucie Inlet and the point of land at modern North Palm Beach.

---

5   We are grateful to Bruce S. Chappell, archivist at the University of Florida's P.K. Yonge Library of Florida History, for helping to decipher these place names.

6   True, "Some Early Maps," 79.

7   Davis, "Juan Ponce de León's Voyages;" Edward W. Lawson, *The Discovery of Florida and its Discoverer Juan Ponce de León* (St. Augustine, 1946); Samuel Eliot Morison, *The European Discovery of America, the Southern Voyages* (New York, 1974), 502-516; Robert S. Weddle, *Spanish Sea, the Gulf of Mexico in North American Discovery, 1500-1685* (College Station, Texas, 1985), 38-54.

8   Davis, "Juan Ponce de León's Voyages," 18.

9   *Ibid.,* 22

Further south there appears what could be a large inlet emptying into the Atlantic and fed by three streams. According to True, geographer Louis Scisco interpreted this to be Jupiter Inlet, the only coastal inlet with "three branching streams at its head."[10] True, however, interprets the feature to be Lake Okeechobee, knowledge of which was presumably conveyed to Juan Ponce by Florida native people.

South of that feature is still another cape, *c[abo] de setos*. In medieval Spanish *setos* may be translated as "poles, fence, or enclosure," suggesting Cabo de Setos may be "Cape of Fish Weirs." Immediately to the south of that cape is *abacoa*, the native village Herrera calls *Abaioa*, near where the expedition anchored in the lee of the cape. According to True, Scisco suggests that town was near Fort Worth inlet.[11]

Southward down the coast the map shows *Rio salado* and *chequiche*. The former, literally Salt River, is said by Scisco to be the New River.[12] Chequiche is, of course, Tequesta, the native village at the mouth of the Miami River known from the Pedro Menéndez de Avilés era. Calling it *Chequescha*, Herrera says the expedition reached that town on its return voyage from the southwest Florida coast.

The efforts by True and Scisco to correlate the Freducci map's Florida place names with locations on a modem map of the Florida Atlantic coast should not be accepted unquestioned, nor should Frederick Davis's interpretation of the Herrera account. The Freducci map, and certainly the latitudes given in the Herrera account, are not exact enough for us to correlate definitely 16th century place names with modem maps. We can just as easily offer an alternative interpretation of that same portion of the Freducci map, one that is no more certain than those of True and Davis.

According to our alternative interpretation, Juan Ponce's initial landfall could have been north of the St. Johns River on one of the barrier islands of southeast Georgia or northeast Florida. The River of Canoes, whose mouth is shown on the Freducci map, could have been the St. Johns River. If correct, then the unlabeled cape just south of the river mouth would probably be on Anastasia Island.

The two capes farther south (near the words Chantio and ponta de Arcifes) could be: (1) the cape just north of Cape Canaveral, named False Cape on

---

[10]   True, "Freducci Map," 51
[11]   *Ibid.*
[12]   *Ibid.*

various Florida maps; and, (2) Cape Canaveral itself. Rather than being the name of the first of these two capes, Chantio could be the name of a native village near that cape, perhaps the village at Turtle mound. Turtle Mound is a very tall shell mound (called Surruque in later Spanish accounts), which served early Spanish sailors as a navigation marker. The second cape, the ponta de Arcifes, would be Cape Canaveral.

The large inlet thought by Scisco to be Jupiter Inlet could instead represent both St. Lucie Inlet and Lake Okeechobee. The latter may have been accessible by native dugout canoe from that inlet. Farther south on the map is Cabo de Setos, in our interpretation the name given modern Miami Beach, below which is Biscayne Bay. Abacoa could be a native village on Key Biscayne, a village represented by one of the large shell middens that still were present on that key in the early 20th century.

The Rio Salado could have been the Miami River itself or the inland waterway that lies between the mainland and the beach islands of northern Dade County. Chequiche was the native town Tequesta, known to have been at the mouth of the Miami River where extensive shell middens also were once present. The Spanish geographer Juan López de Velasco described that setting in his 1575 *Geographía y Descripción Universal de las Indias*:

> At the very point [of land] of Tequesta there enters into the sea a freshwater river, which comes from the interior, and to all appearances runs from west to east. There are many fish and eels in it. Alongside it on the north side is the Indian settlement that is called Tequesta, from which the point takes its name.[13]

The identification of Chequiche (Tequesta) with the mouth of the Miami River seems firm. Placement of all the more northerly names on the Freducci map remain uncertain, although some of the names do seem to be placed north, perhaps well north, of Cape Canaveral.

The Herrera account records that after sailing south along the Atlantic coast of Florida, the Juan Ponce expedition sailed south and westerly along the Florida Keys. Those islands are labeled *los matires* and shown on the Freducci map in their proper location. Here is a second firm geographical correlation with a modern location.

---

[13] John H. Hann, *Missions to the Calusa* (Gainesville, 1991) 314.

On the southwest Florida coast in the general region of modern Fort Myers Beach, the Freducci map provides two place names. The southernmost is *stababa,* a location not mentioned in Herrera. Stababa, a native word, was probably the name for Estero Bay. Most modem archaeologists agree that the village called Calos, the capital town of the Calusa Indians who were encountered by Juan Ponce's expedition, was located on Mound Key, a small island in the bay. Today the large mounds and shell middens of Calos, once home to the Calusa Indians and their pre-columbian ancestors, can still be seen on Mound Key.

Hernando de Escalante Fontaneda, who was shipwrecked in southern Florida in 1545 and lived there more than twenty years before writing a memorial about the south Florida native people, referred to what was apparently the same location, a place he called *Estanapaca.*[14] In 1575 López de Velasco described this place, calling it *Escampaba*:

> The Bay of Carlos, which is called Escampaba in the language of the Indians . . . appears to be the same one that is called, of Juan Ponce, because he landed in it. . . . It is at 26 ½ plus degrees [latitude; it actually is at 26 degrees 24 minutes north latitude]. Its entrance [Big Carlos Pass] is very narrow and full of shoals, as a consequence of which only [small] boats are able to enter. Within it is spacious, about four or five leagues in circumference, although all subject to flooding. There is a little island [Mound Key] in the middle that has a circumference of about a half league, with other islets around it. On this (island) Cacique Carlos had his headquarters and presently his successors have it there (as well).[15]

Father Juan Rogel, a Jesuit missionary priest among the Calusa, wrote a letter in 1568 in which he used the same name, Escampaba, to refer to the Calusa Indian capital.[16] This would appear to be a third Freducci place name which can be tied to a modern place.

The second place name is in southwest Florida on the Freducci map is *guchi* or *juchi,* another Calusa Indian town. That name is placed on the map

---

[14] John E. Worth, "Fontaneda Revisited: Five Descriptions of Sixteenth-Century Florida," *Florida Historical Quarterly* 73 (January, 1995), 348.
[15] Hann, *Missions,* 311-312.
[16] *Ibid.,* 237.

just north of stababa, perhaps near Punta Rassa or in a nearby location. Neither the Caloosahatchee River or Charlotte Harbor are depicted on the map. If indeed the Freducci map depicts the extent of Juan Ponce's initial voyage, then he apparently did not reach either of those places, also suggested by their absence from the Herrera account.

Juchi is a Calusa Indian town that also appears in the writings of Fontaneda. It is mentioned in Fontaneda's well known *Memoir* and in a second document now shown by anthropologist John Worth to have been written by Fontaneda and originally attached to the Memoir.[17] Like the majority of the other Freducci place names, its exact location is uncertain.

On the return voyage from the southwest Florida coast, Herrera records several other place names, names which also appear on the Freducci map. One is an island named by the Spaniards *Matanca* where a battle was fought with the Calusa Indians and where the Spaniards took on water. On the Freducci map *yslas de matanca* is located southwest of stababa and juchi. It could be any of the many islands along the coast.

Next, according to Herrera, the Spaniards sailed to *Las Tortugas*. Those islands, *yslas de tortugas,* are also depicted on the Freducci map in their correct location west of the western end of the Florida Keys.

Two islands at the eastern end of the keys are labeled on the Freducci map: *cambeia* (the southernmost) and *el nirda. Cambeia* is almost certainly the *Achecambei* of Herrera's account.

Did Freducci base his cartographic depiction of Florida on recent accounts or maps derived from the 1513 Juan Ponce de León expedition? It seems likely that he did, although that source may have been a different one from the source or sources Herrera used in writing his account.

If it is accepted that the Freducci map does indeed portray the geography of Juan Ponce's Florida voyage, it provides strong evidence that: (1) the expedition made landfall north of Cape Canaveral; and, (2) the expedition encountered the Calusa Indians in the general Fort Myers Beach—Estero Bay locality and did not explore farther north along the coast. As noted by True, the Freducci map may be the earliest known accurate European depiction of peninsula Florida. As such, it is worthy of more scholarly attention.

---

[17] Worth, "Fontaneda Revisited," 349; David O. True. ed., *Memoir of D. d'Escalante Fontaneda respecting Florida, Written in Spain, about the Year 1575* (Coral Gables, Florida, 1945), 30. In the *Memoir* True renders this as Tuchi; Worth, having seen the original manuscript, notes that Juchi is correct; Worth, "Fontaneda Revisited," 349.

Contemporary Perspectives

Juan Ponce de León and the Indies

Eugene Lyon and Brandon Josef Szinável

2013

Apart from Florida, the place most associated with Juan Ponce de León is San Juan, Puerto Rico. There stands his statue and his burial place in the Cathedral. It appears, however, that Juan Ponce de León had his origins in Spain connected with both branches of his family—in the north, in the present province of Valladolid, and in the south, in Andalucia.

Tracing the genealogy of the Florida adelantado, Juan Ponce de León, is made difficult by the large number of illegitimate children in the family in the 15th and 16th centuries. However, the Spanish Ministry of Culture has made available data about Ponce de León's parents from Madrid's *Archivo Histórico Nacional* that can be accessed through the source *Wikipedia*[1].

The surname "Ponce de León" dates from the 11th century and the first person from whom truly we trace our Florida discoverer was his grandfather, Juan Ponce de León y Ayala. This man, the second Count of Arcos, was born in Villagarcía de la Torre, and died in 1469. His son, Lope Ponce de León, married Catalina de Perea Carrizosa. Their son, Juan Ponce de León González de Perea, born in 1450 in Santeverás de Campos, Spain, was the *Adelantado* of Florida. As a soldier, he participated in the *Reconquista* of Spain from the Moors, being present with Christopher Columbus at its final act, the surrender of Granada. Young Juan Ponce departed for the Indies (the Spanish name for the Americas) in 1493 as part of the second discovery voyage of Columbus. Although no muster roll exists for that voyage, royal historian Gonzalo Fernández de Oviedo y Valdés affirms Juan Ponce's presence aboard.[2]

After that, he must have returned fairly quickly to Spain, for he is shown to have sailed westward again as part of Nicolás de Ovando's 1502 voyage.

---

[1] See Document 87, Writ authorized by Juana Ponce de León, wife of Pedro de Porras, in favor of Rodrigo Ponce de León, III Count of Arcos and his nephew, Juan Ponce de León, son of Lope Ponce de León and Catalina de Perea over certain items she concedes—house and donations in Utrera. Archivo Histórico Nacional, Sección Nobleze, Sgnatura Osuna.

[2] Oviedo y Valdés, Gonzálo de. *Historia general y natural de las indias, islas y tierra-firme del mar océano* . 14 vol. (Asunción, Paraguay: Editorial Guarani, 1944), 3:193-194.

Ovando had been sent to replace Francisco Bobadilla as governor of Hispaniola. After the city of Isabella was abandoned in favor of the permanent capital of Santo Domingo, Spaniards spread out across the island seeking land, slaves and gold.

Once the young Juan Ponce was back in Hispaniola, he wasted no time in coming to the attention of its governor. In the 1504 war in Higüey, in the southeastern section of the island, he performed so well that that he was granted more than 200 acres of land, with Taino laborers to work it, and the title of *Adelantado* of that province. Juan Ponce built a town named Salvaleón. His large stone house still stands there. By raising cassava, sweet potatoes and other vegetables, hogs and cattle, Juan Ponce prospered by sales to ships passing by. Soon he was a wealthy man.

But the young Castilian remembered the lovely green island of San Juan Bautista (called by the island natives Boriquén) when it had been sighted during Columbus's second voyage. Ship-captains told him more about it. He wanted to return there, and perhaps did in 1506. Certainly in 1508 he had returned to San Juan Bautista and built a town about ten miles from present-day San Juan. There followed a period of years in which Juan Ponce served a number of offices in Puerto Rico, ending as governor in 1511, but he was removed from office when Diego Columbus won back his father's rights in the island. The King's royal commissioner in Hispaniola, Miguel de Pasamonte, suggested to Juan Ponce de León that he apply for rights in unknown territories to the north of Hispaniola, called *Beimini*. Columbus's brother, Bartolomé Colón, created a map in 1506 showing Asia lying to the northwest of the Bahamas and Cuba, and he also applied to explore for *Beimini*. But Juan Ponce won out and, on February 23, 1512, he received a royal contract for the exploration, settlement and government of "Beimini."[3]

This was a typical conquest-contract, or *adelantamiento*, in which the subject agreed to fulfill certain royal requirements and pay the whole cost of the expedition, except for that of fortresses. In return he would become *Adelantado*, make key salaried appointments, and receive a share of hoped-for profits—all a 16th-century Spanish noble could dream of.[4]

---

[3] See *Colección de documentos inéditos relativos al descubrimiento, conquista, y organización de las antiguas posesiones españolas de América y Oceanía, sacadas de los archivos del Reinos y muy especialmente del de Indias.* 42 vol (Madrid: Real Academia de la Historia, 1864-84), 22:26-32.

At last, on March 4, 1513, Juan Ponce de León sailed from San Juan Bautista for Beimini. He took three ships, with about fifty persons, including one woman. The flagship, *Nuestra Señora de la Consolación* was accompanied by two smaller vessels, the *Santiago* (evidently a caravel) and the *San Cristóbal*, a *bergantín*.

The location of Juan Ponce de León's landing in Florida has long been a subject of debate. Works written in the late 19th and early 20th centuries put the location in St. Augustine, where there is a thriving attraction named the Fountain of Youth Park, built by Walter B. Fraser. It contains an early mission and Native American burial ground, a half-covered coquina cross, and a sulphur-water flow-well. Attendees at the attraction are offered a drink from the well, supposedly Ponce de León's Fountain of Youth. A local historian, Edward W. Lawson, teamed up with Fraser to write a book proclaiming that the property was the first landing-place of Juan Ponce.[5]

The royal historian Antonio de Herrera y Tordesillas is our best source for the first Florida voyage of Juan Ponce de León.[6] Robert Fuson believed that Herrera evidently wrote with the first-voyage log in front of him when he made his account of the expedition. Herrera's account, however, was not published until 1601(and much later in English translation), or about eight decades after the death of Ponce de León. When James Kelley, Jr., an excellent modern Spanish archival scholar, made his translation of Herrera, he was able to furnish a matrix for tracing the route of the expedition.[7]

Now it appeared that the currents of history had begun to run against Edward Lawson's theory that St. Augustine was Ponce de León's landing place. Neither was Robert Fuson's suggested landing place of Palm Coast correct.[8] Sailing his yawl, Captain Douglas T. Peck followed Kelley's translation of the Herrera log from Puerto Rico through the Bahamas to Florida[9].

---

4   For an example of the terms, conditions and implications of an *adelantimiento*, those relating to King Philip II and Pedro Menéndez de Avilés in 1565, see Eugene Lyon, *The Enterprise of Florida* (Gaineville: University Press of Florida, 1976), 45-55.

5   Lawson, Edward W. *The Discovery of Florida and its discoverer, Juan Ponce de León* (Nashville, Tenn.: Cullom and Ghertner, 1946).

6   Herrera y Tordesillas, Antonio de. *Historia General de los hechos de los castellanos en las islas y tierra firme de el Mar Océano.* 10 vol. (Asunción, Praguay: Editorial Guarania, 1945), 2: 207-212.

7   Kelley, James E. Jr. "Juan Ponce de León's Discovery of Florida: Herrera's narrative revisited," *Revista de Historia de America,* 1991, (3):31-36, Instituto Panamericano de Historia.

According to Peck, Juan Ponce probably landed where he did, near Melbourne Beach in Brevard County on April 3, 1513. Since it was Easter-tide and the land he had found was covered with spring flowers, he named it *La Florida*. This landing place has now been accepted by most modern historians, including Michael V. Gannon and Eugene Lyon[10].

From there Juan Ponce's expedition followed Florida's east coast southward and around the Keys to the southwest coast. At Pine Island near present-day Charlotte Harbor the Spaniards landed and skirmished with the Indians, and finally departed, sailing back through the Dry Tortugas and returning to Puerto Rico.

In what was probably the most important achievement of Juan Ponce's discovery voyage, his pilot Antón de Alaminos discovered the mighty north-setting Gulf Stream which approaches Florida closest at Manalapan in present-day Palm Beach County. In 1492, Christopher Columbus had sailed from Palos in Andalusia to the Canary Islands and then west to the Bahamas. But on his return to Spain he had had to fight his way northward from the Greater Antilles to catch westerly winds. The discovery of the Gulf Stream, called by the Spaniards the *Canal de Bahamá,* greatly assisted return voyages across the Atlantic. It pushed ships quickly northward beyond Bermuda to reach strong westerly winds and return more rapidly to Europe. This circular path to America and back was thereafter used by Spain for three hundred years. As the treasures from Mexico and from the silver mines of Potosí in Alto Perú poured into Spanish coffers, the way to bring them home had been established by Ponce de León's pilot.

There are many interconnections between the family of Juan Ponce de León and other families and persons of importance in the Spanish Indies.[11] His paternal grandmother, Teresa de Guzmán, was Lady of the House of Toral, which may explain his service as page or squire to Don Pedro Núñez

---

8   Fuson, Robert H. *Juan Ponce León and the Spanish Discovery of Puerto Rico and Florida* (Blacksburg, Va.: The McDonald & Woodward Publishing Company, 2000), 114.

9   Peck, Douglas T. "Reconstruction and Analysis of the 1513 Discovery Voyage of Juan Ponce de León," *Florida Historical Quarterly*, 1992, 71(2):133-154.

10   Gannon, Michael V. ed., *The New History of Florida* (Gainesville: University of Florida Press, 1996), 18.

11   Szinável, Brandon Josef. "Intersection of Adelantado Don Juan Ponce de León and his descendants that married other Conquistadors, Governors and prominent families." (Port St. Lucie, Fla.: Self-published, 2012).

de Guzmán, brother of the Lord of Toral. His first marriage was to his cousin Doña Leónor Suárez Ponce de León. With his first wife, Juan Ponce had four children:

Don Luis Ponce de León y Ponce de León, born in Salvaleón de Higüey, became a priest in San Juan.[12]

Doña Juana Ponce de León y Ponce de León, born in Salvaleón de Higüey, married Don García Troche de Monroy in September 1526 in San Juan. He was a native of Olmedo near Valladolid, Spain, and served as mayor of San Germán, Puerto Rico.[13]

Doña María Ponce de León y Ponce de León married Don Gaspar Troche de Monroy in 1524 in San Juan. He was a native of the village of Olmedo near Valladolid.[14]

Doña Isabel Ponce de León y Ponce de León married Don Antonio de la Gama, governor of Puerto Rico from 1519 to 1524, and again from 1525 to 1529. They had no children.[15]

The adelantado Juan Ponce de León contacted his cousin Doña Francisca Ponce de León, the second Duchess of Arcos, for funds to help him finance his Florida expedition. She was the daughter of Don Rodrigo Ponce de León, first Duke of Arcos and a major hero of the Reconquest. This appears to connect the Florida adelantado with both branches of the Ponce de León family.[16]

Juan Ponce's second wife, Juana de Pineda, was from Sevilla. She was the daughter of Diego de Melgarejo, who later sued the grandchildren and other descendants of Juan Ponce over his estate.[17] As a result, Don Luis Cristóbal Ponce de León, the second Duke of Arcos, in August 20, 1536, held 202,000 *maravedis* of the property of adelantado Don Juan Ponce de León.[18]

---

[12] Cuesta y Camacho, David Enrique, and Dr. Adolfo Pérez Comas, *Juan Ponce de León, el Adelantado.* (San Juan, Puerto Rico: Hereditas Revista de Genealogía Puertorriqneña, (Vol. 8, No. 2, 2007), 11.

[13] *Ibid.*

[14] *Ibid.*

[15] *Ibid.*

[16] Marquez de la Plata, Vicenta María and Luis Valero de Bernabe, *El Libro de Oro de los Duques* (Madrid: Ediciones Iberoamericanos, SL, 1 Edição, 1994), 58.

[17] See Cubenas, José A., *Spanish and Hispanic Presence in Florida from the Discovery to the Bicentennial* (Miami: Editorial Mensaje, 1979), 55-57.

[18] Balseiro, José Agustín, ed. *The Hispanic Presence in Florida.* (Miami: E.A. Seeman Publishing, 1977).

The Years Between the Voyages

The time between Ponce de León's first and second voyages was eventful in Europe and the Americas. When he returned to Spain, Juan Ponce was knighted and given his own coat of arms. He was now Don Juan Ponce de León. The King proceeded to issue him a second contract, this time for "the island of Bimini" and "the island of Florida." This contract was much the same as the first, but Juan Ponce was now obligated to read to the Indians the *Requerimiento*. This remarkable statement, cobbled together by Spanish religious leaders, reads as follows:

On the part of the King, Don Fernando and Doña Juana, his daughter, Queen of Castile and León, subduers of the barbarous nations, we their servants notify and make known to you as best we can, that the Lord our God, Living and Eternal, created the Heavens and the Earth, and one man and one woman, of whom you and we and all the men of the world, are descendants, and all of those who come after us. But on account of the multitude which has sprung from this man and this woman in the five thousand years since the world was created, it was necessary that some men should go one way and some another, and that they should be divided into many kingdoms and provinces, for in one alone they could not be sustained.

Of all these nations, God Our Lord gave charge to one man, called Saint Peter, that he should be Lord and Superior of all the men in the world, that all should obey him, and that he should be head of the whole human race, wherever men should live, and under whatever law, sect or belief they should be; and he gave him the world for his kingdom and jurisdiction . . .

One of these pontiffs who succeeded that Saint Peter as Lord of the world in the dignity and seat which I have before mentioned, made donation of these isles and mainland to this aforesaid King and Queen and to their successors Our Lords, with all that there is in those territories, as contained in certain writings . . . which you can see if you wish . . .

So Their Highnesses are kings and lords of these islands and mainland by virtue of this donation, and some inhabitants (of those islands) and almost all of those to whom this has been notified, have received and served Their Highnesses as their Lord and King in the way that subjects ought to do, with good without any resistance, immediately, without delay, when they were informed of the afore-said facts. And also they received and obeyed the priests whom Their Highnesses sent to preach to them and teach them our Holy Faith, and all these of their free will without any reward or condition have become Christians, and are so, and Their Highnesses have joyfully and benignantly received them as subjects and vassals . . .

If you do so, you will do well . . . and we in their name shall receive them in love and charity and your wives and your children and your lands, free without servitude . . . and they shall not compel you to turn Christian unless you yourselves, when informed of the truth, should wish to be converted to the Holy Catholic Faith . . . and besides this, their Highnesses award you many privileges and exemptions, and will grant you many benefits.

But if you do not do this, and maliciously delay in it, I certify to you that, with the help of God, we shall powerfully enter into your coun-try and shall make war against you in all ways and manners that we can, and shall subject you to the yoke and obedience of the Church and of their Highnesses; we shall take you and your wives and chil-dren, and make slaves of them, and shall sell and dispose of them as their Highnesses shall command, and shall take away your goods, and do you all the mischief and damage that we can, as to vassals who do not obey . . . and we protest that the deaths and losses that shall accrue from this are your fault and not their Highnesses, or ours.[19]

In addition to the *Requerimiento*, Juan Ponce's new contract obligated him to undertake a punitive expedition against the Caribs, warrior tribes who raided the Tainos in the Caribbean. He did attack the Caribs on Guade-loupe but did not linger there.

Upon his return to the Indies, Juan found that the island of San Juan Bau-tista had been renamed Puerto Rico. In the meantime, in 1519, Hernán Cor-tés had undertaken his famous expedition against the Aztec kingdom of Mexico, which he named New Spain. His pilot was Antón de Alaminos. In

---

[19]   Helps, Sir Arthur. *The Spanish Conquest in America,* 4 vols. (New York: Harper & Brothers, 1856-58), I: 264-67

that same year, Alonso Álvarez Pineda sailed the coasts of the Gulf of Mexico, finding the great Mississippi River. Although at the time of the signing of Juan Ponce's second contract Florida was still considered an island, a map made by Pineda showed that it was a peninsula, part of the North American mainland. Now and ever thereafter, Florida was so identified.

In the same year as Pineda's voyage, Juan Ponce's first wife died, and he remarried to Juana Pineda. They must have required religious approval for marriage, for Juan Ponce's second wife was distantly related to him.

The Second Voyage

Little is known of the ships or men in Ponce de León's second voyage to Florida. We do know that he departed Puerto Rico with two small vessels about February 20, 1521. The best source is Gonzalo Fernández de Oviedo,[20] who characterizes the expedition as one outfitted for settlement, agriculture and stock-raising. Because the narrative states that the temperature was very disagreeable, Juan Ponce may have gone far north of his former landing place, up perhaps to Apalachee. This is further proven by notations on the 1519 Pineda map, showing that Juan Ponce reached at least as far north as Tampa Bay. At their landing place there occurred a real battle with the Indians about July 1, 1521, in which several Spaniards were seriously wounded, including Juan Ponce himself with an arrow-wound to his thigh. Taken to the vicinity of Havana, he died.

It is now time to deal with the myth of the Fountain of Youth. It appears now that not only the St. Augustine attraction but that the whole chimera of a Fountain is rather easily debunked by tracing it to its origin. This appears to have been an Arabic romance of Alexander the Great published in medieval France as *Roman d'Alexandre*.[21] Further, and later, the letter of Prester John describes a miraculous spring which restores youth to the aged.[22]

---

[20] Oviedo y Valdés, Gonzalo Fernández de. *Historia General y natural de las India, isles y tierra firme del mar océano,* 14 vol. (Asunción, Paraguay: Editorial Guarania, 1944), 10: 256-259.

[21] Armstrong, E.C. *The Medieval Roman d'Alexandre,* 2 vol. (Princeton: Princeton University Press, 1935).

[22] Wright, John K. *The Geographical Lore at the time of the Crusades* (New York: Basic Books), 88.

This phantasm was transported to the New World by Peter Martyr, who, in describing the voyage of Juan de Solís, places the "spring whose waters restore youth to old men" on an island of "Boyuca."[23]

Gonzalo Fernández de Oviedo y Valdés stated that Ponce de León sought the healing fountain because he was impotent. This is patently false, for Juan Ponce fathered four children during the period of his life in Puerto Rico and Florida. Moreover, it appears that Juan Ponce took his mistress along on his first Florida expedition.[24]

Another account comes from Hernando d'Escalante Fontaneda, an Indian captive of the Calusa who was rescued by Pedro Menéndez de Avilés on the lower southwest Florida coast in February 1566.[25]

In 1575 he wrote his *Memoir*,[26] linking Juan Ponce's alleged search for the rejuvenating waters to the Jordan River in Florida (the Jordan River was actually located in present-day South Carolina). Garcilaso de la Vega ("El Inca") in his work translated as *Florida of the Inca* states that Juan Ponce did seek a restorative fountain.[27]

An 1849 book written by Washington Irving picked up the work of Herrera about Ponce de León and enhanced and romanticized the legend of the Fountain of Youth.[28]

Robert H. Fuson's biography of Juan Ponce describes his search for the Fountain as a significant motive for his expeditions in that he was doing that for the aging King Ferdinand, who had just married a young queen.[29]

Connections of the Family of Juan Ponce De León

23   Martyr d'Anghiera, Peter. *De Orbe Novo: The Eight Decades of Peter Martyr d'Anghiera*. Translated by Francis A. MacNutt, 2 vols. (New York: Burt Franklin, 1970).

24   See Peck, Douglas T. *Ponce de León and the Discovery of Florida* (St. Paul, Minn.: Pogo Press, 1993), 25-26.

25   See Eugene Lyon, *The Enterprise of Florida* (Gainesville: University of Florida, 1976), 148.

26   Hernando d'Escalante Fontaneda, *Memoir of Hernando d'Escalante Fontaneda*. Translated by Buckingham Smith, edited by David O. True (Coral Gables, Fla.: University of Miami Press, 1944).

27   De la Vega, Garcilaso. *The Florida of the Inca*. Translated by John G. and Jeannete Varner (Austin: University of Texas Press, 1951).

28   Irving, Washington. *The Life and Voyages of Christopher Columbus* (New York: Putnam Publishers, 1849).

29   Fuson, Robert H. *Juan Ponce de León* (Blacksburg, Va.: The MacDonald & Woodward Publishing Company, 2000), 118-119.

The family and descendants of Juan Ponce de León run through many years of history in the Caribbean and Florida. For example, Doña Francisca Ramos married Don Pedro Menéndez de Valdés, the founder of Manatí, Puerto Rico. She descended from Don Diego Menéndez de Valdés, governor of Puerto Rico from 1581 to 1592 and Doña Elena de Valdés, a distant cousin to her husband.[30] Governor Menéndez de Valdés was a relative to the Adelantado of Florida and founder of St. Augustine, Don Pedro Menéndez de Avilés.[31]

Rodrigo de Bastidas Hoyos, first possessor of the entail of his house married with Juana Fernández de Oviedo, only daughter of Gonzalo Fernández de Oviedo y Valdés, *cronista de Indias*.[32]

A witness to a 1746 wedding in Santo Domingo was Captain Don Francisco de Mieses Ponce de León, who was a descendant of Florida Adelantado Don Juan Ponce de León. Don Francisco's mother was Doña Francisca Pérez Caro y Fernández de Oviedo, a descendant to governor of Santo Domingo Don Rodrigo de Bastidas and Don Gonzalo Fernández de Oviedo y Valdés , royal *cronista*.[33]

Don García de Carvajal y Ponce the son of Alonso de Carvajal and Ana de Carvajal was a passenger on May 6 1604 traveling to Santo Domingo.[34] He served as *regidor* in Santo Domingo as of May 21, 1621, and married Doña Catalina de Burgillos, who was baptized June 18, 1592 in the Cathedral of Santo Domingo as the legitimate daughter of Captain Juan Ortiz de Sandoval, descendant to Don Hernán Ponce de León, a comrade to Don Hernando de Soto and his wife Doña Catalina de Bastidas y de Oviedo. She was a daughter to Don Rodrigo de Bastidas III, second Lord of the mayorazgo of Bastidas and Doña Juana de Oviedo y Valdés, the daughter of Don Gonzalo Fernández de Oviedo y Valdés, the *cronista*.

On August 13, 1565, Pedro Menéndez de Avilés entered the harbor of San Juan, Puerto Rico on his way from Spain to his Florida clash with the Huguenot French. There he met one of the Royal Treasury officials of the

---

30   A.G.I. *Indiferente* 118, No. 118.

31   Vigil, Ciriaco Miguel. *Noticias bigráficas de Pedro Menéndez de Avilés* (Avilés: Miguel Vigil, 1892), 119. (The co-author Brandon Josef Szinável is the fifth great grandson of Don Josef Menéndez de Valdés).

32   Larrazabal Blanco, Carlos. *Familias Dominicanas* (Santo Domingo, Dominican Republic: Academia Dominicana de la Historia, Vol. 1, 1969), 245-246.

33   *Idem.*, Vol. 3, 160.

34   AGI *Pasajeros a Indias, I, 8, E. 2700.*

island, with the same name as the deceased adelantado, Juan Ponce de León. This Juan Ponce received Menéndez' power of attorney and helped him to buy a ship and recruit soldiers for the Florida expeditions.[35]

This is the man known as Juan Ponce de León II, who married Doña Isabel López de Loasia, daughter of former Puerto Rico governor Don Íñigo Ceravanta de Loasia. Juan Ponce II arranged the transfer the remains of his grandfather, Juan Ponce de León, from Cuba and had him buried at the San José church in San Juan, later to be moved to the San Juan Cathedral in 1913.

On the tomb of Juan Ponce de León is inscribed the following:

> . . . the mortal remains of Juan Ponce de León, a native of the land of Campos, whose gallant deeds were evidence of his noble and pure lineage. Soldier in Granada, Captain in Hispaniola, a conqueror and Governor in San Juan del Boriquén, Discoveror and first Governor of Florida; valiant military man, skillful leader, loyal subject, honest administrator, loving father, and industrious colonist. He surrendered his soul to God and his body to the earth in Havana (1521). To his venerable memory and in honor of the Christian civilization introduced through his impetus, founded by his bravery and spread by his diligent cooperation in this bountiful Puerto Rican land, a devout tribute is consecrated.

---

[35] See Lyon, Eugene. *The Enterprise of Florida* (Gainesville: University Press of Florida, 1976), 103-104.

Juan Ponce De León and the Fountain of Youth: History, Myth, and the Commemoration of Florida's Past

J. Michael Francis

2013

History is messy for the people who must live it.[1]

—Michel Rolph-Trouillot

In 1575, not long before his death, a Spaniard named Hernando de Escalante Fontaneda drafted a remarkable memoir, chronicling his seventeen-year ordeal as a captive among Florida's Calusa Indians. Twenty-six years earlier, in 1549, Escalante had survived a shipwreck in the Florida Keys and was rescued and taken in by the Calusa. At the time, he was just thirteen years old.

Escalante's brief narrative provides some of the richest ethnographic evidence available for the Calusa Indians and other southern chiefdoms, and is widely considered one of the most important documents on early-colonial Florida history.[2] But the account is perhaps best known for another story. Escalante's memoir includes one of the earliest written references to Florida's most enduring foundation myth, Juan Ponce de León and his quest for the Fountain of Youth. According to Escalante, Indians from Cuba and Santo Domingo were convinced that a magical river existed somewhere on the Florida peninsula. They believed that bathing in the sacred water from this river turned old men young again. For that reason, Escalante continued, large numbers of Indian migrants had fled Cuba for south Florida, where they spent their days in search of the elusive waters.

---

[1] Trouillot, Michel-Rolph, *Silencing the Past: Power and the Production of History* (Boston: Beacon Press, 1995), 110.

[2] Hernando de Escalante Fontaneda's original account of Florida's southern chiefdoms is housed at the *Archivo General de Indias* (hereafter, AGI) in Seville, Spain. See "Relación sobre Florida," AGI Patronato 19, R. 32, and "Descripción de las islas Bahamas," AGI Patronato 18, N. 5, R. 1.

Escalante then proceeded to deride the Indians for believing such a foolish legend, the search for which had caused the death of so many Indians. He explained that while he was a captive he had bathed in many of Florida's numerous rivers; yet "to my great displeasure," Escalante added with a hint of sarcasm, "I was never able to verify the fountain's existence." He then mocked the lone Spaniard naïve enough to believe such a tale: Juan Ponce de León. "It was simply laughable" that Juan Ponce de León would set out on such a quest to discover the location of this river.

It might be easy to understand Escalante's contempt for Ponce if it were not for one small matter: it is largely untrue. Juan Ponce de León was never searching for a Fountain of Youth. There, I said it . . . Ponce de León was never searching for a Fountain of Youth.

Of course, Escalante did not invent the Fountain of Youth fable, nor was he the first to associate Ponce de León with the quest to find it. Rumors of magical rejuvenating springs had deep historical roots in medieval lore, occupying a privileged place in Eurasian mythology, along with tales of Amazon women, the Seven Cities of Cíbola, and other popular tales. Versions of these stories had long existed in many parts of Europe, the Middle East, and Asia. Thus, it is hardly surprising that not long after Columbus's initial voyages to the Caribbean, reports began to emerge that the elusive waters were to be found somewhere in the New World.

Perhaps the earliest reference to a New World fountain of youth can be found in the account written by Peter Martyr d'Anghera (1457-1526), a Milanese humanist who resided at the Spanish court. Martyr never traveled to the Americas, but he had access to official reports and numerous eye-witness testimonies. Writing to the pope in 1514, Martyr reported rumors of a magical spring that turned old men young again. According to the reports, the river was situated 325 leagues from Hispaniola (far from the Bahamas or Florida), and the witnesses insisted that when old men drank from its water, combined with some specific diet, they turned young again. Martyr claimed that the story had already spread throughout the Spanish court and that many wise and wealthy men believed it to be true. Yet Martyr dismissed the rumors, arguing that only God had such power to transform the old into young men again. Not only was Martyr deeply skeptical of the story, but it should also be noted that he never connected the myth to Ponce de León or to Florida for that matter. In fact, at the time he wrote the letter, Martyr was likely unaware of Ponce's 1513 voyage. At the time, "Florida" did not even exist.

It was not until the mid-1530s, more than two decades after Ponce de León's initial voyage to Florida, and more than ten years after his death, that Ponce de León first became associated with the quest for the Fountain of Youth. In 1535, the great Spanish chronicler Gonzalo Fernández de Oviedo y Valdés (1478-1557) published the first fifteen (of fifty) 'books' of his magisterial *Historia general y natural de las Indias*, an exhaustive work of human and natural history, widely considered the finest chronicle of the sixteenth century. In it, Oviedo praised the actions of men like Christopher Columbus and to a lesser extent, Hernando Cortés; however, he also vilified the greed, capriciousness, superstition, and stupidity of others. One of his targets was Juan Ponce de León. According to Oviedo, Ponce was a vain and credulous man, prone to pursue silly ventures that enhanced his own ego, no matter the cost. To illustrate his point, Oviedo related a story that Ponce had allegedly been told by a group of Indians in the Caribbean. He claimed that the Indians had deceived Ponce and his followers, leading them to believe that an enchanted spring was hidden somewhere in the islands of Bimini (the Bahamas), and that its waters made men young again. Convinced the rumors were true, Oviedo claimed, Ponce and his men wandered aimlessly among the islands for six months.

Continuing his assault on a credulous Ponce, Oviedo added that he himself had witnessed first-hand how old men could turn young, which he claimed occurred without the assistance of any fountain. Rather, the transformation was caused simply by a weakening of the brain, which made grown men behave like young boys of little reason or understanding. This, Oviedo claimed, was precisely what had happened to Ponce de León. Only Ponce's own vanity, Oviedo concluded, could explain how he could have believed such a foolish tale and embark on a quest that proved so costly in material and human resources.[3]

If Oviedo initiated the link between Ponce de León and the search for the fabled fountain, another Spanish chronicler, Antonio de Herrera y Tordesillas, reinforced the connection. Herrera's 1601 chronicle, *Historia de los hechos de los Castellanos en las islas i tierra firme del mar oceano*, provides the most detailed account of Ponce's 1513 voyage and appears to have been

---

[3] For Oviedo's account of Juan Ponce de León's 1513 expedition, see Gonzalo Fernández de Oviedo y Valdés, *Historia general y natural de las indias, islas, y Tierra Firme del Mar Océano*, Tomo II, Libro XXVI, Cap. I, (Madrid: Imprenta de la Real Academia de Historia, 1853), 621-623.

based in part on now-lost original accounts of the expedition. Often labeled as one of the great plagiarists of the early-modern era (a practice that was in fact common among virtually all early modern chroniclers) Herrera borrowed liberally from previous chroniclers such as Oviedo.[4] It is highly likely he was also aware of Escalante's captivity narrative, as Herrera's version of the Fountain of Youth story bears a striking resemblance to Escalante's rendering.

Since the publication of Herrera's chronicle, scores of modern writers have repeated, distorted, and often exaggerated, the historical association between Ponce's 1513 expedition and the Fountain of Youth. Over time, what began as myth has slowly transformed into historical fact. Still, it is important to recognize that nowhere in Ponce de León's known correspondence does he mention the Fountain of Youth or a quest to find it. Likewise, Ponce's 1512 contract (*capitulación*) with King Ferdinand, which detailed the terms of the expedition, makes no reference to a search for the legendary waters.[5] When the contract was amended two and half years later, there was still not mention of it. In fact, there are no references to the Fountain of Youth in any of the original documents associated with Ponce's 1513 voyage or his return to Florida in 1521.

If he was not searching for a fountain of youth, why then, did Ponce embark on such a costly expedition? Simply put, Ponce wanted to be compensated for having been forced to surrender the governorship of Puerto Rico in 1511. With no political future in Puerto Rico or Cuba, Ponce had to seek fame and fortune elsewhere. Rumors of rich islands to the northwest of Puerto Rico led the disgruntled Ponce to negotiate the rights and privileges for a new conquest expedition, and like so many of his contemporaries, he expected these new territories to yield wealth, titles, power, and prestige. He was never searching for a magical elixir that promised to restore his youth.

Of course, I am not the first historian to challenge the veracity of the Fountain of Youth story and its connection to Ponce de León's expeditions to Florida. Over the past century, numerous scholars have attempted to dismantle the narrative, all to little avail. In a lengthy article published in 1935

---

[4] Herrera y Tordesillas, Antonio de, *Historia general de los hechos de los castellanos en las islas i tierra firme del mar océano*, Decado I, Libro IX, Cap. X – XII (Madrid: Imprenta Real de Nicolás Rodríguez Franco, 1729), 246-252.

[5] "Asiento con Juan Ponce de León," AGI Indiferente 418, L.3, (February 23, 1512), fols. 253r-255v.

in the *Florida Historical Quarterly*, T. Frederick Davis blamed modern writers for falsely connecting the Fountain of Youth story with Ponce de León's 1513 voyage to Florida, which Davis claimed elevated the popular myth "to an importance far greater than it deserves historically."[6] Four decades later, in 1965, the very year that St. Augustine celebrated its 400-year anniversary, Luís Rafael Arana not only contested the claim that Ponce's expedition had been organized to search for the fabulous spring, but he added that there was absolutely no evidence that Ponce was even aware of the story.[7] Still, the story persisted, another instance where myth trumps history. And still, the scholarly attacks continued.

In 1992, Douglas T. Peck blasted previous historians for "perverting" the "factual past" in favor of the Fountain of Youth fable. For Peck, the fabled spring belongs in the realm of folklore and fantasy.[8] Likewise, Robert Fuson, author of one of the few recent English-language biographies of Ponce de León, lamented that Ponce was "best remembered for something he did not find—a magic fountain, the pursuit of which was not even his idea." (Unfortunately, Fuson implied that King Ferdinand ordered Ponce to search for the rejuvenating spring, a claim for which there is no supporting evidence).[9] Most recently, Tony Horwitz's witty satire, *A Voyage Long and Strange on the Trail of Vikings, Conquistadors, Lost Colonists, and Other Adventurers in Early America*, presented the Fountain of Youth story as one of many contemporary historical hoaxes, aimed not to inform, but rather to entertain, deceive, and relieve unsuspecting tourists of their spending money.[10]

In early April of 2013, Floridians across the state will gather to commemorate the 500-year anniversary of Juan Ponce de León's landing. Local, state, and federal organizations, as well as educational institutions, tourism offi-

---

6   Davis, T. Frederick, "History of Juan Ponce de León's Voyages to Florida," *The Florida Historical Society Quarterly*, Vol. 14, No. 1 (July, 1935), 47.

7   Arana, Luis Rafael, "The Exploration of Florida and Sources on the Founding of St. Augustine," *The Florida Historical Quarterly,* Vol. 44, No. ½, Quadricentennial Edition (July-October, 1965), 4-5.

8   Peck, Douglas T., "Misconceptions and Myths Related to the Fountain of Youth and Juan Ponce de León's 1513 Exploration Voyage," (New World Explorers, Inc.), 4-18. A full text of this paper can be accessed at www.newworldexplorersinc.org/FountainofYouth.pdf.

9   Fuson, Robert H., *Juan Ponce de León and the Spanish Discovery of Puerto Rico and Florida,* (Blacksburg, VA: The McDonald & Woodward Publishing Company, 2000), 118-120.

10   Horwitz, Tony, *A Voyage Long and Strange: On the Trail of Vikings, Conquistadors, Lost Colonists, and Other Adventurers in Early America*, (New York: Picador, 2008), 284-286.

cials, and businesses, are busy planning programs, conferences, and promotions aimed to attract visitors to the state and to share Florida's rich but often neglected colonial past. But what exactly are the stories we are going to tell? And who is going to tell them?

Ponce de León and the Fountain of Youth tale will undoubtedly figure prominently in the commemoration celebrations of 2013. As Florida's most enduring popular myth, it probably should. In fact, one might argue that the tale has become so deeply woven into the fabric of Florida's collective identity that it has now transcended myth. It has become an integral part of Florida's past, especially over the last 150 years. I think there is some truth to that claim, and I do not advocate a campaign to dismantle it. We can learn a great deal from studying myths, how they evolve and transform, and why they persist. At the same time, the inherent danger in any commemoration celebration is that myth will overshadow history. In the end, the central problem with fables such as the Fountain of Youth is that they tend to simplify and trivialize the past.

The upcoming commemoration celebrations provide a unique opportunity to move beyond myth, to share Florida's real past. From the earliest contact in the sixteenth century, Florida's history became part of a global tale, one that extended into the vast Caribbean, across the Atlantic to the Iberian Peninsula and the rest of Europe. It became intimately connected to Africa and the slave trade, and goods from Asia circulated throughout the province, beginning in the sixteenth century. And despite their declining numbers over the three centuries of colonial rule, Florida's disparate Indian populations always outnumbered Europeans and Africans. For more than three centuries, European, African (both free and enslaved), and Indian men and women interacted. And like all human affairs, their relationships were complex and messy. At various times, Florida's early inhabitants fought, negotiated, traded, competed, celebrated, married, raised families, exploited, and cohabited. Violent clashes occurred, but so did long periods of peace and coexistence, alliances and intermarriages. Tragedy blended with triumph, and events often unfolded in unpredictable ways, with surprising outcomes. Ultimately, Florida's "real" history is far richer and, dare I say it, entertaining, than the mythical tale of an aging conquistador on a failed quest to locate a magical river, whose restorative waters would bring him good health perpetual youth. We know the myth; it's time to share the history.

Scholars' and Storytellers' Visions of Juan Ponce de León: Two Centuries of Work

Amanda J. Snyder

2013

Five centuries ago, Juan Ponce de León, a seasoned soldier, left Spain in search of new frontiers. As a "gentleman volunteer," he joined Christopher Columbus' second voyage to the Caribbean in 1493. In the following centuries, this soldier-turned-explorer and his expeditions would become the stuff of legend. Popular literature surrounding Ponce de León emphasizes the quest for the mythical Fountain of Youth and, at times, the scholarly literature has certainly indulged in this tradition. Both made it their goal to canonize the Spanish explorer. This essay briefly touches on the wealth of literature surrounding Ponce de León's La Florida expedition to illuminate some of the greater debates of myth and the lasting impact of Ponce de León's endeavours.

A member of Spain's noble Guzmán family, Ponce de León earned a name for himself in the Moorish campaigns of the 1490s. After fighting in the Granada campaign, helping the Spanish crown re-conquer land in southern Spain, Ponce de León looked for the next opportunity to put his military skills to use. Like many men of the time, that opportunity lay across the Atlantic Ocean in the newly-'discovered' lands of the Americas. In the Caribbean, Ponce de León served as a provincial governor in Hispaniola, fought the indigenous Tainos of Puerto Rico, and served as governor following the pacification of the island. His next journey, though, would become his most famous.

In 1513, Ponce de León made his first voyage to La Florida—the expedition that has received the most scholarly and popular attention. Contemporary accounts related that Ponce de León was searching for healing waters around Beniny, but, it was not until after his death that his Florida and Caribbean expeditions became tied to the mythical Fountain of Youth. No eye-witness accounts survive from this mission. In 1601, seventy years after the Florida explorations, Antonio de Herrera compiled the first published accounts of Ponce de León's voyages in *Historia General de los Hechos de los Castellanos en las Islas y Tierra Firme del Mar Oceano*. Sixteenth-century writings such as Gonzalo Fernández de Oviedo's *Historia General y*

Natural de las Indias (1535) and Francisco López de Gómara's *Historia General de las Indias* (1552), the first comprehensive histories of Spanish America, mention Ponce de León as well, but not in as much detail as is dedicated to his fellow explorers. In fact, even in modern scholarship, Ponce de León is overshadowed by Christopher Columbus, Hernán Cortes, and Francisco Pizarro. Although some modern works mention Ponce de León, only recently has he become a more noteworthy figure of study in and of himself. This renewed interest is clearly attributable to the quincentennial anniversary of his Florida expeditions. Despite this fact, the majority of works that discuss Ponce de León are not focused primarily on the man himself. They are part of larger studies of early modern Spanish explorers, the American conquests, and the process of Spanish American colonization.

Today, a search for the Spanish explorer shows that interest in promoting the Fountain of Youth predominates, even though most historians agree that there is little evidence of this fantastic voyage. The fabled Fountain of Youth has become a favourite topic of children's books' authors and Hollywood directors. Because these books remain so popular, historians have consistently worked to discover the origins and veracity of this connection and to discover the true aims and character of Juan Ponce de León. Even so, the mythical Fountain of Youth remains but one aspect of the Ponce de León literature. Reflecting changes in scholarly trends, the academic canon now also includes detailed research into Ponce de León's route and the day-to-day events of his voyage and exploration.

Early in the 20th century, the myths surrounding the Fountain of Youth began to be challenged by an increasing cohort of professionalized historians. T. Frederick Davis' *History of Juan Ponce de León's Voyages to Florida*, one of the most cited works on Ponce de León during the early 20th century, tackles the veracity of the legend.[1] Other historians, like Leónardo Olschki sought to connect legend and history. In his 1941 article, "Ponce de León's Fountain of Youth: History of a Geographical Myth," Olschki drew upon contemporary sources to connect Ponce de León to the Fountain of Youth.[2] Using Peter Martyr's *De Orbo Novo Decades* (1530) as his starting

---

[1] Davis, T. Frederick, "History of Juan Ponce de León's Voyages to Florida," *The Florida Historical Society Quarterly*, Vol. 14, No. 1 (July, 1935).

[2] Leónardo Olschki, "Ponce de León's Fountain of Youth: History of a Geographical Myth," *Hispanic American Historical Review* 21, no. 2 (May 1943): 165–96.

point, Olschki argues for the "irrefutable evidence of an attested historical tradition" regarding the famous fountain.[3] Many of Davis' and Olschki's Spanish contemporaries, like Aurelio Tió and Vicente Murga Sanz, devoted little attention to the Fountain of Youth's association with Ponce de León. Tió's and Murga Sanz's works actively followed an agenda dedicated to promoting the Hispanic point of view.

More recently, scholar Luis Arana sought to discover the origin of the myth itself, namely that the Fountain of Youth myth became connected with Ponce de León in Spain rather than in the Americas. Arana states that even though rumours about the fountain circulated in Spain as early as 1514, only in 1535 did Gonzalo Fernández de Oviedo connect the rumours to Ponce de León. These rumours spread and became so exaggerated that by the end of the century Herrera declared the search as the true aim of Ponce de León's exploration despite any contemporary evidence to this fact.[4]

Douglas Peck examined the "natural, though misguided" connection of Ponce de León and the Fountain of Youth that began in early modern European histories.[5] Peck points out that the original charters for Ponce de León's voyages had no mention of the Fountain, nor could significant firsthand accounts be found to substantiate the discovery of the Fountain as the expeditions' primary goal. By the mid-20th century, scholars were re-translating the chronicles and diaries surrounding Ponce de León's voyages in order to more clearly separate the explorer from legend and grounding him in the reality of American exploration. Among these were extensive historical and archaeological studies to determine Ponce de León's exact navigations and landings in La Florida—the name that he himself gave to the lands he discovered. Detailed debates resulted from the works over the exact landing points of Ponce de León's ships. Even now, these debates seem to be without complete resolution. J. Denucé (1910), L. D. Scisco (1913), Luis Arana (1965-1966), and David O. True (1954) were some of the scholars who scoured the archives and contemporary journals to map out the La Florida expedition and its stops.[6] In a review of Samuel Morison's two-volume work *The Great Explorers: The European Discovery of America* (1978), Charles Arnade weighed in on some of these authors' debates. Morison disputed

---

4   Luis Arana, "The Exploration of Florida and Sources on the Founding of St. Augustine," *Florida Historical Quarterly* XLIV (July 1965-April 1965–66): 4–5.

5   Douglas T. Peck, *Ponce de León and the Discovery of Florida: The Man, the Myth, and the Truth* (St. Paul, MN: Pogo Press, 1993), 4.

True's claims that the English explorers, the Cabots, were actually the first to sight Florida. Morison accepts Tio's assertions that Ponce de León discovered the Mexican coast as well as Florida—an assertion disputed by most historians.[7] In 1992, Douglas Peck went so far as to recreate the voyage attempting to use the same instruments as the Spanish explorer and his crew. Peck claims that Ponce de León never found Beniny, but that his navigations of the Gulf Stream proved even more vital to Spanish exploration than the discovery Beniny would have been.[8]

Archaeological studies like Kathleen Deagan's *Artifacts of the Spanish Colonies of Florida and the Caribbean, 1500-1800* and Deagan's and José Mariá Cruxent's *Archaeology at La Isabella: America's First European Town* contribute to these debates and help to illuminate the world in which Ponce de León operated.[9]

In the 1970s and 1980s, studies focused on Ponce de León's relationship with the indigenous groups he governed in Puerto Rico and those he encountered on his expeditions throughout the Caribbean and American southeast. Antonio Stevens-Arroyo's *Cave of the Jagua: The Mythical World of the Tainos* and Jerald Milanich and Susan Milbrath's *First Encounters: Spanish Explorations in the Caribbean and the Unites States, 1492-1570* are some of the earlier works to focus on indigenous relations.[10] Stevens-Arroyo examines the mythology and religion of the Taino people.

---

[6]   J Denucé, "The Discovery of the North Coast of South America According to an Anonymous Map in the British Museum," *The Geographical Journal* 36, no. 1 (July 1910): 65–80; L. D. Scisco, "The Track of Ponce de León in 1513," *Bulletin of the American Geographical Society* 45, no. 10 (1913): 721–35; David O. True, "Some Early Maps Relating to Florida," *Imago Mundi* 11, no. 1954 (1954): 73–84; Peck, "Reconstruction."

[7]   Charles Arnade, review of The Great Explorers: The European Discovery of America, *Florida Historical Quarterly* (1978): 222

[8]   Peck, "Reconstruction," 154.

[9]   Kathleen Deagan, *Artifacts of the Spanish Colonies of Florida and the Caribbean, 1500–1800*, drawings by James H. Quine (Washington, D.C.: Smithsonian Institution Press, 1987); Kathleen Deagan and José María Cruxent, *Archaeology at La Isabela: America's First European Town* (New Haven: Yale University Press, 2002).

[10]   Antonio M. Stevens-Arroyo, *Cave of the Jagua: The Mythological World of the Taínos* (Albuquerque, NM: University of New Mexico Press, 1988). Jerald T. Milanich and Susan Milbrath, eds., *First Encounters: Spanish Explorations in the Caribbean and the United States, 1492–1570*, Ripley P. Bullen Monographs in Anthropology and History, no. 9 Columbus quincentenary series (Gainesville: University of Florida Press: Florida Museum of Natural History, 1989).

His discussion delves into the "feminine" organization of Taino religion and society, claiming that such an organization could not withstand the masculine civilization brought by the Spanish. Milanich and Milbrath's collection, and the museum exhibit that accompanied it, stressed the effects of European disease and Spanish wars of conquest on the native populations.

Irving Rouse continued in this tradition and also addressed the effects of the Columbian Exchange in Puerto Rico with his study *The Tainos: Rise and Decline of the People who Greeted Columbus*.[11] All these books built upon renewed research interest in "borderlands" studies begun largely by Herbert Bolton in his classic study on *The Spanish Borderlands: A Chronicle of Old Florida and the Southwest* (1921).[12] A part of a multi-volume history on the Americas, Bolton's work remains a cornerstone of early borderland and frontier historiography. Bolton's work was one of the first to focus on a Hispanic past for America, rather than the standard English discovery tropes. His student, John Francis Bannon revived the work with his *The Spanish Borderland Frontier, 1513-1821* (1970) and rekindled interest in such research.[13]

As for Ponce de León himself, biographies range from Berdine Richman's 1919 anthology entry in *The Spanish Conquerors: A Chronicle of the Dawn of Empire Overseas*, to Manuel Ballesteros' 1987 *Juan Ponce de León* to Aurora Venturini and Fermín Chávez's 1999 *Ponce de León y el fuego*.[14] Robert Fuson's *Juan Ponce de León and the Spanish Discovery of Puerto Rico and Florida* draws on first-person accounts of the La Florida voyages.[15] Working from early chronicles such as the Herrera compilation, Fuson attempts to demythologize Ponce de León and his voyages. Fuson's work,

---

11   Irving Rouse, *The Tainos: Rise and Decline of the People Who Greeted Columbus* (New Haven: Yale University, 1993).

12   Herbert E. Bolton, *The Spanish Borderlands: A Chronicle of Old Florida and the Southwest* (New Haven: Yale University, 1921).

13   John Francis Bannon, *The Spanish Borderlands Frontier, 1513–1821* (Albuquerque: University of New Mexico, 1974).

14   Berdine Richman, *The Spanish Conquerors: A Chronicle of the Dawn of Empire Overseas*, The Chronicles of America Series, vol. 2 (New Haven: Yale University, 1919); Manuel Ballesteros, *Juan Ponce de León*, Protagonistas de América (Madrid: Historia 16: Quorum, 1987); Aurora Venturini and Fermín Chávez, *Ponce de León y el Fuego* (Bs. As. [i.e. Buenos Aires: Corregidor, 1999).

15   Robert H. Fuson, *Juan Ponce de León and the Spanish Discovery of Puerto Rico and Florida* (Blacksburg, Va.: McDonald & Woodward, 2000).

while important for pushing for new translations of the earlier histories, has been taken to task by reviewers. Paul Hoffman criticizes the Puerto Rican hagiographic tradition regarding the explorer that pervades Fuson's narrative. Even so, the book remains one of the better, more comprehensive biographies of Ponce de León. The bibliography following this essay includes some two dozen biographies of Ponce de León (though this is meagre compared to studies of other Spanish explorers and conquistadors of his time).

To better understand the context in which Ponce de León operated students must look to Carla Rahn Philip's translation of Spanish historian Pablo Pérez-Mallaína's work, *Spain's Men of the Sea: Daily Life on the Indies Fleet in the Sixteenth Century.*[16] This work details sailors' motivations for embracing sea voyages, their wages, and their accounts of life on ship, in the New World, and back in port in Seville. Waxing romantic at times, the study is useful for historians of early exploration. Pérez-Mallaína offers context for Ponce de León that Fuson, and others, neglect. *Spain's Men of the Sea* is one among many Age of Sail histories, but is specifically tied to the famous port of Seville and the men with whom Ponce de León sailed.

Despite the amount of literature written about the early Florida expeditions, we can still easily ask Charles Arnade's question of "Who Was Juan Ponce de León?"[17] An intrepid explorer, comrade to Columbus, and governor of Puerto Rico, Ponce de León gathered valuable information about navigating the Gulf Stream and discovered some of most useful harbours on the Florida coast for future Spanish explorers. The history of Ponce de León is more than the Fountain of Youth and more than just a side note among Spanish conquistadors. This collection will fill one void for more in-depth studies and reinterpretations of the La Florida voyages and their place among the first New World explorations.

---

[16] Pablo E. Pérez-Mallaína, *Spain's Men of the Sea: Daily Life on the Indies Fleets in the Sixteenth Century*, Trans. Carla Rahn Phillips (Baltimore: Johns Hopkins University Press, 1998).

[17] Charles Arnade, "Who Was Ponce de León?" *Tequestia*, no. XXVII (1967): 29–58.

A Bibliography of Works about Juan Ponce de León and The Florida Voyages

Amanda J. Snyder

2013

Allen, John Logan, ed. *North American Exploration*. Lincoln: University of Nebraska Press, 1997.

Bailey, Bernadine. *Juan Ponce de León: First in the Land*. Illustrated by Cheslie d'Andrea. Boston: Houghton Mifflin, 1958.

Ballesteros Gaibrois, Manuel. *La Idea Colonial de Ponce de León; un Ensayo de Interpretación*. San Juan, P.R.: Instituto de Cultura Puertorriqueña, 1960.

Ballesteros, Manuel. *Juan Ponce de León*. Protagonistas de América. Madrid: Historia 16: Quorum, 1987.

Bolton, Herbert E. *The Spanish Borderlands: A Chronicle of Old Florida and the Southwest*. Yale Chronicles of America Series. Toronto: Glasgow, Brook, and New York: United States Publishers Association, 1977.

Brown, G. M. *Ponce de León Land and Florida War Record*. St. Augustine, Fla., 1902.

Brown, George M. *Ponce de León Land*. St. Augustine, Fla.: The Record Printing Co., 1901.

Davis, Frederick. *History of Juan Ponce de León's Voyages to Florida: Source Records*. Jacksonville: Fla., 1935.

Devereux, Anthony Q. *Juan Ponce de León, King Ferdinand, and the Fountain of Youth*. St. Augustine, Fla.: Florida Historical Society, 1993.

Fairbanks, George R. *History of Florida from Its Discovery by Ponce de León, in 1512, to the Close of the Florida War, in 1842*. Philadelphia: J.B. Lippincott, and Jacksonville, Fla.: C. Drew, 1871.

Fraser, Walter B. *The First Landing Place of Juan Ponce de León on the North American Continent in the Year 1513*. St. Augustine, Fla., 1956.

Fuson, Robert H. *Juan Ponce de León and the Spanish Discovery of Puerto Rico and Florida*. Blacksburg, Va.: McDonald & Woodward Pub. Co., 2000.

Greenberger, R. *Juan Ponce de León: The Exploration of Florida and the Search for the Fountain of Youth.* The library of explorers and exploration. New York: Rosen Pub. Group, 2003.

Harwood, John, and Kirsten Miller, eds. *Florida Stories: Tales from the Tropics.* San Francisco: Chronicle Books, 1993.

Irving, Washington. *Voyages and Discoveries of the Companions of Columbus.* Paris: Baudry, 1831.

Kenny, M. *The Romance of the Floridas; the Finding and the Founding.* With a foreword by Dr. James A. Robertson. Science and Culture Series, J. Husslein, General Editor. New York, 1934.

Kerby, E. P. *The Conquistadors.* Illustrated by J. Polseno. A World Pioneer Biography. New York: Putnam, 1969.

Kerrigan, Anthony. *Barcia's Chronological History of the Continent of Florida from the Year 1512, in Which Juan Ponce de León Discovered Florida, Until the Year 1722.* Translated by Herbert B. Bolton. Westport: Conn.: Greenwood Press, 1970, c1951.

King, Ethel. *The Fountain of Youth and Juan Ponce de León.* Brooklyn: T. Gaus' Sons, 1963.

Lawson, Edward W. *The Discovery of Florida and Its Discoverer Juan Ponce de León.* St. Augustine, Fla.: E. W. Lawson, 1946.

Lawson, Edward W. *Determination of the First Landing Place of Juan Ponce de León on the North American Continent in the Year 1513.* St. Augustine, Fla.: Florida Historical Society, 1954.

Lowery, Woodbury. *The Spanish Settlements Within the Present Limits of the United States, 1513-1561.* New York: Russell & Russell, 1959.

Milanich, Jerald T., and Susan Milbrath, eds. *First Encounters: Spanish Explorations in the Caribbean and the United States, 1492-1570.* Ripley P. Bullen Monographs in Anthropology and History, No. 9, Columbus Quincentenary Series. Gainesville: University of Florida Press/Florida Museum of Natural History, 1989.

Moscoso, F. *Bibliografía de la conquista y colonización de Puerto Rico: Siglos XV-XVII (1492-1650).* San Juan, P.R.: Universidad de Puerto Rico, Recinto de Río Piedras, Departamento de Historia, 2005.

Murga Sanz, Vicente. *Juan Ponce de León: Fundador y Primer Gobernador del Pueblo Puertorriqueño, Descubridor de la Florida y del Estrecho de las Bahamas.* San Juan: Ediciones de la Universidad de Puerto Rico, 1959.

Otfinoski, S. *Juan Ponce de León: Discoverer of Florida*. Great Explorations. New York: Benchmark Books, 2003.

Peck, Douglas T. *Ponce de León and the Discovery of Florida: The Man, the Myth, and the Truth*. Florida: Pogo Press, 1993.

Peters, Virginia Bergman. *The Florida Wars*. Hamden, Conn.: Archon Books, 1979.

Reynolds, Charles B. *The Landing of Ponce de León; a Historical Review*. Mountain Lakes, N.J., 1934.

Richman, Berdine. *The Spanish Conquerors: A Chronicle of the Dawn of Empire Overseas*. The Chronicles of America Series, Vol. 2. New Haven: Yale University Press, 1919.

Richman, Irving Berdine. *Adventurers of New Spain*. New Haven: Yale University Press, 1926.

Rubio, Juan Luis Carriazo, and prólogo de Miguel-Angel Ladero Quesada. *La Memoria del Linaje: Los Ponce de León y sus Antepasados a Fines de la Edad Media*. Serie Historia y Geografía, No. 73. Sevilla: Universidad de Sevilla, Ayuntamiento de Marchena, 2002.

Schmidt-Nowara, C. *The Conquest of History: Spanish Colonialism and National Histories in the Nineteenth Century*. Pitt Latin American Series. Pittsburgh, Pa.: University of Pittsburgh Press, 2006.

Saínz Sastre, María Antonia. *La Florida, Sigo XVI: Descubrimiento y Conquista*. Madrid: Editorial MAPFRE, 1991.

Slavicek, L. C. *Juan Ponce de León*. The Great Hispanic Heritage. Philadelphia: Chelsea House, 2003.

Stefoff, R. *Accidental Explorers: Surprises and Sidetrips in the History of Discovery*. Extraordinary Explorers. New York: Oxford University Press, 1992.

Thompson, Bill and D. Thompson. *Real Adventure with the Discoverers of America: Leif Ericson, Christopher Columbus, Ponce de Léon, Ferdinand Magellan*. Exploration and Discovery. Philadelphia, Penn.: Mason Crest, 1954.

Vallvé, Manuel. *Juan Ponce de León, Descubridor de la Florida*. Ilus. de J. De La Helguera. Los Grandes Hechos de los Grandes Homres. Barcelona: Editorial Araluce, 1930.

Venturini, Aurora, and Fermín Chávez. *Ponce de León y el Fuego*. Buenos Aires: Corregidor, 1999.

Weber, David J. *The Spanish Frontier in North America*. The Lamar Series in Western History, 2009.

Weddle, Robert S. *Spanish Sea: The Gulf of Mexico in North American Discovery, 1500-1685*. College Station: Texas A&M University Press, 1985.

Winter, Nevin O. *Florida, the Land of Enchantment; Including an Account of Its Romantic History from the Days of Ponce de León and the Other Early Explorers and Settlers, and the Story of Its Native Indians; a Survey of Its Climate, Lakes and Rivers and a Description of Its Scenic Wonders and Abundant Animal and Bird Life; and a Comprehensive Review of the Florida of to-Day, as a State Important for Its Industries, Agriculture and Educational Advantages as Well as the Unsurpassed and Justly Celebrated Winter Resort of America, with Unparalleled Attractions for Health and Pleasure Seekers, Nature Lovers*. Motorists and Sportsmen by Nevin O. Winter. See America First Series. Boston: The Page Company, 1918.

Wright, E. Lynne. *It Happened in Florida: Remarkable Events That Shaped History*. It Happened in Series. Guilford, Conn.: Globe Pequot Press, 2010.

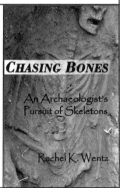

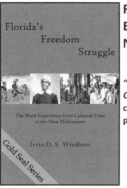

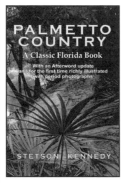